MUSICAL ARCHITECTS

MUSICAL ARCHITECTS

CREATING TOMORROW'S ROYAL ACADEMY OF MUSIC

ROYAL
ACADEMY
OF
MUSIC

UNICORN

CONTENTS

INTRODUCTION

When Professor Jonathan Freeman-Attwood took over as Principal of the Royal Academy of Music in 2008, he was determined to fine-tune the curriculum and consolidate the position of the Academy in the top rank of conservatoires. By the time this book was written in 2020, the new energy in the Academy was palpable, and the already impressive list of teaching staff had exciting names added, with an enviable catalogue of internationally renowned visiting professors. Squeezed into prestigious but challengingly crowded buildings, from the Academy's creation in 1822 this world leader among music colleges has seen a subtle but vitally important renaissance. Corridors buzz with itinerant young people of all nationalities tucked into any available spaces to concentrate on making music.

The Academy's prospectus is stimulating and the programmes of study and performances, public concerts and highly professional recordings formidable. The challenges facing musicians today are ever more exacting and the Academy aims to send its graduates into a supremely competitive environment with a musical training that gives them the best chance to use their individual talents in an unforgiving world, and with the experience and life skills needed for them to survive and hopefully flourish.

Musical Architects is a celebration of the Academy's energy and dynamism as it approaches its bicentenary in 2022, and of the central role played by the skilful designing of a new theatre and recital hall. Early in 2020, as the final layouts of this book were being approved, the coronavirus pandemic engulfed the world and the Academy fell silent. As I write, young musicians are showing their ingenuity and jointly creating online music, adapting to a strange environment.

Appreciation of our buildings, both new and old, will increase as a result of this exceptional hiatus. The Academy – ever resourceful – will continue to innovate and thrive. It is a powerhouse producing music of all genres and honing the talents of over 800 students at any given moment to provide an extraordinary musical patchwork that resonates strongly. With a remarkable ability to absorb new directions as successfully as it interprets the world's vast musical legacy, the Academy reveals its relevance to the modern world as much as to its historical roots.

Jonathan Freeman-Attwood had been Vice-Principal before he took on the leadership role and had ample opportunity to examine the Academy's operations and create a master plan to prepare the institution for an ambitious but attainable future.

Early one morning in February 2009, I walked with Jonathan into the Sir Jack Lyons Theatre at the Academy. He had been Principal for just a few months, but was moving with considerable vigour to examine the need for change and improvement. He had realised that the excellent and increasingly notable Opera Department, and the small but flourishing Musical Theatre Department, lacked a performance space that enabled them to demonstrate adequately the skills of the students and the results of the outstanding training they were receiving.

Although we did not know it then, we were about to embark on a roller-coaster journey that ended triumphantly in March 2018 with the opening of two exceptional new performance spaces. The addition of a startlingly beautiful state-of-the-art theatre and sublime recital hall has provided facilities that have sharpened the ambitions

Opposite and following pages:
Roof of the Angela Burgess
Recital Hall

of the entire Academy, and laid down a marker showing that the organisation is ready to take on new challenges and retain relevance for its remarkably talented students as it approaches its bicentenary.

Our close look at the Sir Jack Lyons Theatre that cold spring morning was depressing. It was 'landlocked' in the centre of the grand Edwardian and neoclassical sprawl of the Academy. Built in 1976 with generous support from Sir Jack Lyons, it had been squeezed pragmatically into the only space available and was compromised from the outset by the lack of a fly tower and usable wing space, and simply did not have adequate technical facilities for high-quality performance.

By 2009 the theatre was drab and its inadequacies in terms of sight lines, acoustics, accessibility and an impossibly small orchestra pit made it a disappointing space for student performances in an increasing range of theatrical disciplines. Miracles were performed there, but it was evident that better facilities were vital. It was also clear that tinkering with the existing space was likely to be an expensive cosmetic gesture that would not produce the fundamental changes we needed, but embarking on a major reconstruction was a huge undertaking that would stretch the resources – human and financial – of the entire organisation. I had been closely involved in a number of capital arts projects

(including the £100 million transformation and rebuilding of the Royal Shakespeare Theatres in Stratford-upon-Avon) and knew just what a comprehensive drain such developments can be.

In 2001 the Academy had enhanced its teaching facilities with the valuable addition of the 130-seat recital venue, the David Josefowitz Recital Hall, linking the main building with the 1998 acquisition of 1–5 York Gate. There was an unshakeable belief that it was impossible to make radical improvements to the existing theatre. But the inescapable fact was that a conservatoire of serious standing unable to provide appropriate facilities to display the talents of the flourishing Opera and Musical Theatre Departments would be unsustainable and uncompetitive, nationally and internationally.

The Governing Body of the Academy – led by the far-sighted Chairman, Lord Burns – accepted the need for a complete transformation of the Sir Jack Lyons Theatre, and a group of Governors, chaired by Matthew Ferrey, became the embryonic Theatre Working Group that would eventually see the project through. Soon the process of conducting a feasibility study leading to a comprehensive programme of work was under way, and the Development Department began to be aware of the huge fundraising challenge that lay ahead. Few Governors or members of staff at the Academy had any experience of a capital project. And no one had any idea of the complexities of managing such major construction in the middle of a fully functioning educational establishment of nearly a thousand students, active seven days a week, and with the non-negotiable requirement for extended periods of silence on-site to allow for auditions, recitals and exams. It was hard to imagine a more daunting prospect.

We had asked the architect Ian Ritchie to join us on our exploratory walk-round in early 2009, and after the initial feasibility study the Governing Body invited him to tackle the unenviable task of presenting a scheme for a viable theatre complex in the centre of the Academy, where the only access for construction would be through the roof, and ideally providing extra practice percussion studios and practice rooms, better circulation and proper disabled access. And all this to be delivered within an acceptable time frame and a manageable budget.

Ian Ritchie already had a considerable reputation for assessing a client's ambition and requirements and finding solutions that were ingenious, effective and – unusually – for putting the wishes of the client before the whims of the architect. It is almost impossible to identify a 'Ritchie' building: each one is designed to fit the purposes and personality of the organisation. His immensely varied use of materials and deep understanding of design, engineering and technology enables him to surprise and delight again and again. Often challenging, he has a proud reputation for exploring in depth what a client thinks they want and need, and then moving the agenda forward to deliver an enhanced version of those expressed needs.

As an example, his Sainsbury Wellcome Centre for Neural Circuits and Behaviour is an extraordinary laboratory, built on a constricted site in central London, predominantly clad in cast glass and with entirely adaptable laboratory space, and flexible services that can be reconfigured by the scientists to suit their changing requirements and working methods. Through its spatial organisation it provides a layout that encourages constant interaction between scientists. It alters the paradigm of laboratory design and is the envy of many prestigious scientific institutions across the world. The design was developed from inception in continuous close collaboration with neuroscientists from University College London, and deliberately incorporates knowledge from neuroscience in its planning, fabric and structure.

In work for the Royal Shakespeare Company in Stratford-upon-Avon, Ritchie designed the Courtyard Theatre – a superb, welcoming 1000-seat theatre, opened in 2006, instantly loved by actors and audiences – which was built on a low budget for the RSC to use while the Royal Shakespeare Theatre was being totally rebuilt. Several years later, under Ritchie's guidance, the Courtyard Theatre morphed quietly and astonishingly into a new version of The Other Place. Now the social hub and centre of much of the RSC's life in Stratford, The Other Place houses a fully flexible auditorium, the costume wardrobe, busy rehearsal rooms, and a constantly buzzing café and bar. Ritchie provided the RSC with these new and enticing spaces, entirely fit for purpose and encouraging unforeseen uses of the buildings that have delivered significant and lasting benefits. He understands the atmospheric conditions that allow live performance to develop and flourish. He also understands the physical environment – light, materials and the critical organic relationship between performers and audiences – and how to create places where energy flows. He asks as many questions as he gives answers and options.

Ritchie's approach to the needs of the Academy was no different. He has an uncanny knack of looking at an architectural situation and quickly seeing possibilities that go beyond the brief and deliver much more than the client had imagined or considered feasible.

The Academy had asked for a new theatre and ancillary spaces (which seemed a Herculean task) but, aware that this would be the only remaining opportunity for the institution to generate more space on its constrained site, Ritchie quickly suggested creating more room at roof level directly

above the restructured theatre – with all the difficulties that this could pose with regard to planning permission, constructability and cost. The 'space' that emerged from conversations between the Principal and the architect produced an idea for an astonishing addition to the already ambitious theatre project: a recital hall on the roof. The last available area on the Academy's footprint was the existing roof, with its accumulation of mechanical equipment, above the old theatre, which had never even vaguely been considered usable. Ritchie demonstrated that a new structure perched above, and accessed through the back wall of the Academy's main Edwardian building, would be invisible from the street or from Regent's Park, and would provide an immeasurably valuable additional venue. The costs of the scheme would, of course, rise but the ultimate benefits were inescapable and irresistible. The generosity of John Burgess allowed the construction of the Angela Burgess Recital Hall. It is named after his mother who had been a piano student at the Academy, and it has provided an invaluable and already much-loved extra space.

By the time the project was formally launched in 2012, the Chairmanship had been passed on to Dame Jenny Abramsky. Under her committed leadership construction began in 2015, with the Theatre Management Group bolstered by professional support. The Academy's Senior Management Team knew that all those involved would have to hold their nerve, have great patience and belief in the value of the end game … and raise a lot of money. The potential restrictions and complications in the plans for construction were formidable, and the ambitions for the project verging on the foolhardy, but the enthusiastic anticipation as Ritchie's early ideas emerged was highly contagious and the scope of this complex and awe-inspiring scheme had a pleasing audacity that we were right to embrace, although the journey had some tense moments.

Football played a surprising but important role in the project. Ian Ritchie is a lifelong supporter of Liverpool Football Club, a passion he shares to the same immoderate degree with Jonathan Freeman-Attwood, and over the years in which the project at the Academy occupied our professional lives, that dogged loyalty provided many moments of shared joy and frustration, and created a deep bond that enabled any professional tension to be ridden out with no lasting damage! The precise shade of red chosen for the seats in the theatre auditorium is not accidental.

Throughout the project we benefited from the remarkable dedication of the construction team and subcontractor specialists, and from the exceptional skill and commitment of the design team led by Ian Ritchie Architects. The shared pride and determination of those professionals, and the members of the Academy staff and student body, whose patience was sorely tested, allowed this extraordinary venture to succeed. Indeed, without their constant individual and collective expertise the Academy simply would not have been able to operate.

The response to the finished theatre and recital hall, and the palpable thrill felt each time anyone goes into the dazzling new spaces for the first time, ensures that the moments of anxiety, exasperation and fear that can scar any major capital development have already faded into the ether.

The Susie Sainsbury Theatre and the Angela Burgess Recital Hall were opened officially in March 2018, to universal acclaim and delight, envy and awe. To date the project has won more than twenty major national and international architectural awards, and been commended for a further twenty-four. Most importantly, these exceptional facilities allow the talents of the students to shine, while proudly declaring the Royal Academy of Music's ambitions as it enters its third century.

Susie Sainsbury
Deputy Chairman

LONDON. Royal Academy of Music

A BRIEF HISTORY OF THE ROYAL ACADEMY OF MUSIC

William Crotch (1775–1847)

John Baptist Cramer (1771–1858)

Carl Maria von Weber (1786–1826)

The Royal Academy of Music was founded with visionary zeal on high Enlightenment ideals refracted through a fug of tobacco smoke and a haze of alcohol in London clubs during the summer of 1822. Since the 1760s there had been proposals to set up a national music school to emulate the Paris Conservatoire and the renowned Italian Ospedali – something to mirror the Royal Academy of Arts that had been founded in 1768 – but London's musicians had proved better at talk than action. The new Academy succeeded where so many other plans foundered because it was backed by leading Establishment figures, in a spirit of post-Napoleonic international swagger, who were ardent musical amateurs and capable politicians with strong European connections. Under royal patronage, a committee of peers, government ministers, courtiers and businessmen agreed the purposes of the new institution and oversaw its foundation. In a public announcement

on 21 July 1822 the committee described the object of the Academy as 'to promote the cultivation of Music, and afford facilities for attaining perfection in it'. This mission lay at the core of the Academy's royal charter granted by King George IV in 1830, and two centuries later it still underpins the Academy's goals.

The founding committee appointed Dr William Crotch, Professor of Music at the University of Oxford, as the first Principal. Crotch was required to audition, recruit and instruct up to eighty young musicians – forty boys and forty girls aged between ten and eighteen – and to hire 'the most eminent professors' in the land to teach them. The enterprise was to be funded through the payment of tuition fees and the private philanthropy of subscribers. The Academy was housed at 4–5 Tenterden Street, rented mid-terrace accommodation just south of Oxford Street, which the Academy quickly outgrew. Despite periodic bouts

of internal remodelling, it continued to cramp the young institution's style for the rest of the nineteenth century, accompanied by the constant refrain of neighbours' complaints about the racket.

By the time the first lesson was given on 24 March 1823, Dr Crotch had assembled an impressive teaching staff drawn from London's cosmopolitan musical elite. Many of the professors were émigré musicians with distinguished pan-European careers, such as the pianists Ignaz Moscheles and John Baptist Cramer, soon to be followed by Manuel Garcia (brother of celebrated diva Maria Malibran), one of the Academy's longest-serving professors, who was still teaching on his hundredth birthday; others were English musicians with impeccable European credentials, such as Ludwig van Beethoven's friend Cipriani Potter. From the start, there was an internationalism that continues to characterise the Academy to this day. The young students – among

Cipriani Potter (1792–1871)

Sir William Sterndale Bennett (1816–1875)

the first cohort of whom was Charles Dickens's sister, Fanny – were subjected to a busy daily timetable of instruction that mixed traditional aspects of apprenticeship with some pedagogical experimentation and a startlingly ambitious artistic programme. One of the first public shows was an English adaptation of Wolfgang Amadeus Mozart's *Così fan tutte* (called *Tit for Tat*), which was surprising given the rarity of Mozart's operas in London at the time and the subject matter of this particular piece. Discipline was strict and students had to wear a specially designed uniform: half livery and half military in design for the boys, and for the girls white dresses with red sashes that were still de rigueur well into the twentieth century and are now preserved in the Academy's (men's) soccer strip.

Having a virtual monopoly on advanced musical training in Britain until the 1880s, the Academy exerted an enormous influence on musical practice

and taste throughout the nineteenth century. Leading foreign musicians were attracted into its orbit. Carl Maria von Weber was one of the Academy orchestra's first guest conductors in the 1820s; all Mozart's late symphonies were performed at the Academy in the 1830s; Felix Mendelssohn was a regular visitor in the 1830s and '40s; and Franz Liszt taught at the Academy in the 1880s. There were also some near misses: an attempt to recruit Gioachino Rossini to the staff came close to fulfilment, and Robert Schumann actively pursued the possibility of moving to London to work at the Academy in the 1840s, and dedicated his Symphonic Etudes, Op 13, to his Academy friend and one-time Principal, Sir William Sterndale Bennett. More important than the presence of these figures was the regular programming of their music and other 'novelties' from Germany, France and Italy.

It is amazing how quickly seminal nineteenth-century works found their way

into the Academy's public events, from late Beethoven string quartets to Rossini's *Barber of Seville*. The persistence of older music in the Academy's programmes, especially by George Frederick Handel, Franz Joseph Haydn and Mozart, helped to cement the idea of a classical canon in London's musical life. And in championing the music of another long-dead composer, the Academy showed itself to be in touch with the very latest Continental trends. The music of Johann Sebastian Bach was practically unknown in Britain in the early decades of the nineteenth century. Among the founding professors of the Academy were figures who had encountered some of Bach's music through their Viennese connections: most notably William Crotch and Mozart's former pupil, Thomas Attwood. By the 1830s Bach's name was beginning to appear on Academy programmes, including some of his large organ works played on the organ by Cipriani Potter with the great Italian virtuoso Domenico

Sir Arthur Sullivan (1842–1900)

Dame Myra Hess (1890–1965)

Dragonetti playing the pedal part on his double bass. Later generations of Academicians continued to promote Bach's music. The Bach Choir was the child of Academy alumni; Sir William Sterndale Bennett gave the first English performance of the St Matthew Passion in 1854; Otto Goldschmidt conducted the first British account of the B Minor Mass as late as 1876; and cello professor Alfredo Piatti gave the first performance of the Bach suites outside Germany.

Many Academy students from those pioneering years went on to play significant roles in British musical life, but none had a more profound or lasting influence than Sir Arthur Sullivan. His talent was recognised early, and at the age of fourteen he won the inaugural Mendelssohn Scholarship at the Academy, which was established mainly from the proceeds of benefit concerts given by Jenny Lind, 'the Swedish Nightingale'. The discipline Sullivan honed as a

student stood him in good stead as his operettas conquered the English-speaking world: he continued to do his daily technical exercises just as a performer would practise their scales. It was this technical fluency that enabled Sullivan to lift Sir William Gilbert's telling verses off the page so vividly.

By the end of the nineteenth century the Academy had become a victim of its own success and had outgrown its facilities. Student numbers had expanded six-fold to over 500 and the age range had shifted so that most were older than eighteen. The Academy's educational model had been emulated in the foundation of other music colleges in London (Trinity College of Music in 1872, the Guildhall School of Music in 1880 and the Royal College of Music in 1882). Rivalry between the Academy and the fledgling RCM was particularly acute until, by a happy coincidence, in 1885 the new Principal of the Academy, Sir Alexander Mackenzie, discovered that

he lived opposite the Director of the RCM, Sir George Grove, in Sydenham. The two men became firm friends; intercollegiate relations thawed, and with an eye to raising the standards of music training in the provinces the two institutions jointly founded the Associated Board of the Royal Schools of Music in 1889. But the contrast between the purpose-built premises of the RCM in South Kensington, and the Academy's small and increasingly rickety home in Tenterden Street was a source of increasing embarrassment and led to the search for a new site. A plan to move to Decimus Burton's Colosseum near Regent's Park fell through in the late 1880s, and a project to extend the Tenterden site north to Oxford Street also came to nothing in 1909.

Eventually a site formerly occupied by the St Marylebone Charity School for Girls was secured, straddling the Crown and Howard de Walden Estates, and the architectural partnership of George &

Dame Moura Lympany (1916–2005)

Sir Henry Wood (1869–1944)

Yeates was appointed in January 1910. Sir Ernest George's building rose next to York Gate on the north side of Marylebone Road and was formally handed over to the Academy on 25 September 1911. With the addition of the Duke's Hall in 1912 and a small makeshift theatre in the 1930s, these new premises remained essentially unchanged until the end of the twentieth century. Mackenzie, whose brainchild the move was, had a composer's love of puns and toasted the success of the new building with the words, 'Now is the winter of our discontenterden street made glorious summer by this sun of York Gate', a thought that must have been particularly savoured by the vocal professor, William Shakespeare.

The first sixty years in its new home were a time of consolidation for the Academy, which steadily enhanced its reputation for producing outstanding orchestral players, brilliant concert pianists, successful composers in the classical and popular spheres, and alumni with the force of personality and imagination to play leading roles in national and international musical circles. The renowned piano pedagogue Tobias Matthay taught generations of students, many of whom later became household names, such as Dame Myra Hess, Sir Clifford Curzon, Harriet Cohen and Dame Moura Lympany. Chamber music coaching was in the expert hands of legendary performers like the violist Lionel Tertis and the violinist Sidney Griller. Among the numerous great orchestral players to emerge from the Academy in those years – many of whom were pioneers of the BBC Symphony, the Philharmonia and a whole host of emerging chamber orchestras – pride of place must surely go to the horn player Dennis Brain, whose life ended prematurely in a car crash in 1957.

A rapid rise in the standard of orchestral training from the 1920s onwards was not just due to the professionalisation of London orchestras. Equally important was the magnetic personality of the Academy alumnus Sir Henry Wood. Already a major international figure, synonymous with the promenade concerts ('The Proms') and Britain's greatest champion of new music, from 1924 until his death twenty years later Wood trained the Academy's first orchestra with the same meticulous attention to detail that he brought to his professional concert work. He also attracted a host of renowned European figures as visitors to the Academy, including Richard Strauss who conducted an unforgettable performance of his tone poem *Tod und Verklärung* in the Duke's Hall in 1936. Wood was the first of three Academy alumni to become world-leading conductors despite having studied another discipline, the others being Sir John Barbirolli (cello) and Sir Simon Rattle (percussion). Barbirolli demonstrated some of the

Architectural drawings of the Royal Academy of Music by Sir Ernest George and Alfred Yeates, 1910-11, showing details for the main façade (left) and for the main staircase (right)

R·A·M ½ DETAIL OF STAIRCASE

SECTION SHOWING WINDOWS

SECTION THRO' LANDINGS.

ERNEST GEORGE & YEATES
ARCHITECTS
18 MADDOX ST W.

Sir John Barbirolli (1899–1970)

Sir Colin Davis (1927–2013)

tenacity that characterised his later career when, as a young student, he organised the British premiere of Maurice Ravel's String Quartet in the gentlemen's loos after the Principal had forbade its performance in the Duke's Hall as its loucheness might offend young ladies. Rattle's legendary student performance of Gustav Mahler's Second Symphony, while extracurricular, was at least delivered with official approval. One could, of course, add many others who studied instruments that played only a tangential part in their eventual career path, such as Annie Lennox (flute).

The most significant educational initiative in the inter-war years was undoubtedly the foundation and development during the 1930s of the Junior Academy as a Saturday school for talented musicians under the age of eighteen. Many Junior Academy alumni are just as distinguished as their senior counterparts. Among those who made

their mark in music are the two Middlesex schoolboys who became Sir Elton John and Sir Andrew Davis. But the diplomatic corps, the law, politics, academia and the business world are peppered with individuals whose deep love of music was nurtured at the Academy on Saturday mornings, and who regard the Academy as their alma mater as much as the universities they later attended.

As the twentieth century approached its end, the pace of reform at the Academy accelerated after the strong consolidating years of musical and pastoral direction under Sir Thomas Armstrong and Sir Anthony Lewis. In the 1980s and '90s there were significant developments in the music profession and in British higher education: in both spheres boundaries were broken down and old certainties questioned. Well-established career paths became less secure, but for bold and ambitious musicians with a broad cultural hinterland there

opened up a wider range of artistic and entrepreneurial opportunities. The challenge for the Academy was how to continue to anticipate these trends as much as reflect them, and this period of the institution's history was marked by driven transformation.

In the 1980s Principal Sir David Lumsden established a series of International Chairs held by leading practitioners: Anne-Sophie Mutter (violin), Lynn Harrell (cello), Robert Tear (vocal studies), Christopher Hogwood (early music) and Sir Colin Davis (conducting). Of these distinguished figures, along with the Amadeus Quartet, Davis made the greatest contribution to the institution, conducting the Academy's orchestras and opera productions regularly until his death in 2013 – a commitment rivalled only by Wood and Barbirolli earlier in the century.

A the same time, a series of composer festivals was inaugurated, each dedicated

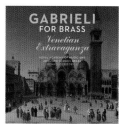

Olivier Messiaen (1908–1992)

Packshots of Academy recordings
on Linn Records

to a major figure who worked intensively with students in preparing concerts of their own music. These festivals read like a roll call of leading composers from the second half of the century: Olivier Messiaen, György Ligeti, Elliott Carter, Luciano Berio, Witold Lutosławski, Krzysztof Penderecki, Hans Werner Henze, Michael Tippett, Arvo Pärt, György Kurtág and the film composer John Williams among others. The real significance of these initiatives was that they set a benchmark not so much for special events at the Academy but rather for its daily life. By the turn of the century the Academy's termly artistic programme took the form of a continuous twelve-week festival with students working side by side on compelling projects with distinguished international practitioners. And the faculty appointments of that period mirror the distinctiveness of the holders of international chairs with a cornucopia of world-renowned teachers.

For example, professors of composition included Sir Harrison Birtwistle, Sir Peter Maxwell Davies and Thomas Adès.

The structure and scope of the Academy's courses were evolving in tandem with, and in some respects ahead of, the changing music profession. The range of subjects offered was increased to include Jazz, Musical Theatre and Commercial Music as well as niche classical disciplines such as Historical Performance, Choral Conducting and Classical Accordion. The breadth of the training regime was expanded to encompass a greater emphasis on the humanities together with the latest trends in musicology and their application to performance and interpretation. An Academy CD label was established by the then Vice-Principal Jonathan Freeman-Attwood, who applied his professional experience as a recording producer to provide students with the opportunity to record and showcase their achievements.

And the Open Academy department was founded to spearhead students' engagement within the wider community and to hone their skills as communicative ambassadors for the power and benefits of music to human well-being and the life well lived. It also became increasingly important to give students the kind of business skills that would enable their artistry to flourish in a competitive professional musical environment. In 1990 a concordat was signed with King's College London to introduce and award an undergraduate degree programme in musical performance for Academy students. This replaced all previous undergraduate diplomas. The King's degree was followed in 1999 by the Academy's accession as a member institution of the University of London. The Academy was granted the power to award its own degrees in 2012.

The new degree programmes were able to draw on unrivalled musical collections.

Grand piano, Giovanni Heichele,
Trieste, c 1815

Oliver Knussen (1952–2018)

From its earliest years the Academy regularly received gifts of instruments, manuscripts and printed materials, and other musical artefacts, which were supplemented by judicious purchases at auction. In the nineteenth century the most significant gift was John Rutson's collection of Cremonese stringed instruments, including a remarkable group of Strads and Amatis. With further outstanding additions in the last thirty years – such as the Beckett Collection and the Calleva Collection – the Academy now has the finest instrument collection of its kind in the world. At the heart of the manuscript collections are some key pieces in Britain's musical identity: Henry Purcell's *The Fairy Queen*, Ralph Vaughan Williams's *Fantasia on a Theme by Thomas Tallis* and Edward Elgar's *In the South*. Surprises sometimes turn up, as when, for example, the only surviving score of Handel's *Gloria* was found within a miscellany of manuscripts at the

Academy. The Academy's collections are particularly rich in the working materials of eminent musicians, including Sir Henry Wood, Sir John Barbirolli, Robert Spencer, David Munrow, Nadia Boulanger, Otto Klemperer, Yehudi Menuhin, Sir Charles Mackerras, Ferenc Fricsay and Oliver Knussen. Complementing these materials are large collections of musical iconography and ephemera, which are rich resources for the annual exhibitions mounted in the Academy's museum.

During the twenty-first century the Academy has continued to evolve rapidly. By 2000 there were more than 700 students, and there are now nearly 900 due to the expansion of the undergraduate programme, and the introduction of Masters programmes, post-Masters diplomas and a PhD programme. Like the old Tenterden Street premises in the late nineteenth century, the Academy's Marylebone home would have struggled with the increased demands of a modern conservatoire

training for such numbers were it not for a series of expansions and new facilities. The York Gate building (housing the Academy's museum and collections as well as teaching and rehearsal facilities for Musical Theatre) and the David Josefowitz Recital Hall came into operation in 2001 under the leadership of Sir Curtis Price.

The refurbished foyer, new practice rooms and an opera studio created in the so-called 'void', the Cross Keys Practice Centre and Aybrook Street teaching building, and the fine Kuhn organ in the Duke's Hall (courtesy of Sir Elton John and his co-alumnus, drummer Ray Cooper) were all added in the early 2010s, under the new Principal from 2008, Jonathan Freeman-Attwood. The installation of state-of-the-art recording facilities in the Academy's public performance spaces has allowed students to curate their online presence with more sophistication, and enabled live events at

Royal Academy of Music foyer

Sir Peter Maxwell Davies (1934–2016)

the Academy to reach global audiences through livestreaming. And, above all, the transformational and award-winning new Susie Sainsbury Theatre and Angela Burgess Recital Hall crowned twenty years of expansion and renovation in 2018, providing Royal Academy Opera and the Musical Theatre Company with a magnificent, incomparable home. At the same time, the entrance to the Academy was radically reimagined to enhance its Edwardian portal and create disabled access.

The first hundred years of the Academy's history coincided with the zenith of the British Empire, and it has long had significant student and staff contingents from Commonwealth countries. But in the current century the global reach of the Academy's international profile has developed enormously, with an ever-increasing diversity in its student and staff populations, underpinned by a busy programme of exchanges, collaborations

and overseas tours. A touring programme began in the 1990s, and the connections with leading institutions in Europe, North America, Asia and Australia have grown and deepened steadily over the last thirty years. Joint research projects have been developed with the Massachusetts Institute of Technology (MIT) and Distinguished Visiting Professorship exchanges set up with Tokyo University of Music and the Arts. But the most enduring international collaboration has been with The Juilliard School in New York, including several concerts with Elton John, three BBC Prom concerts, a tour of Bach cantatas in New York, London and Leipzig under Masaaki Suzuki – a project that emerged from the Academy's celebrated monthly series from 2009 to 2018 (funded by the Kohn Foundation) in which all of Bach's cantatas were performed – a CD of early seventeenth-century Venetian brass music under Reinhold Friedrich,

and the joint commission of a new opera about student protest – *Kommilitonen!* – from Sir Peter Maxwell Davies and Sir David Pountney in 2010. Today, half of the Academy's students come from outside the UK with over fifty countries represented. Alongside this growth in cultural diversity, since 2008 the gender balance has also changed, and is even more striking among the senior staff of the Academy, of whom 70 to 80 per cent are now women.

Collaborations with organisations and artists sharing values of artistic enquiry and excellence have always played a critical part in Academy life. Highlights of the many creative performance opportunities and successful partnerships with the wider industry, from which Academy students benefit today, include major side-by-side performances of iconic contemporary repertoire at London's Southbank Centre with the London Sinfonietta under figures such as Sir George Benjamin,

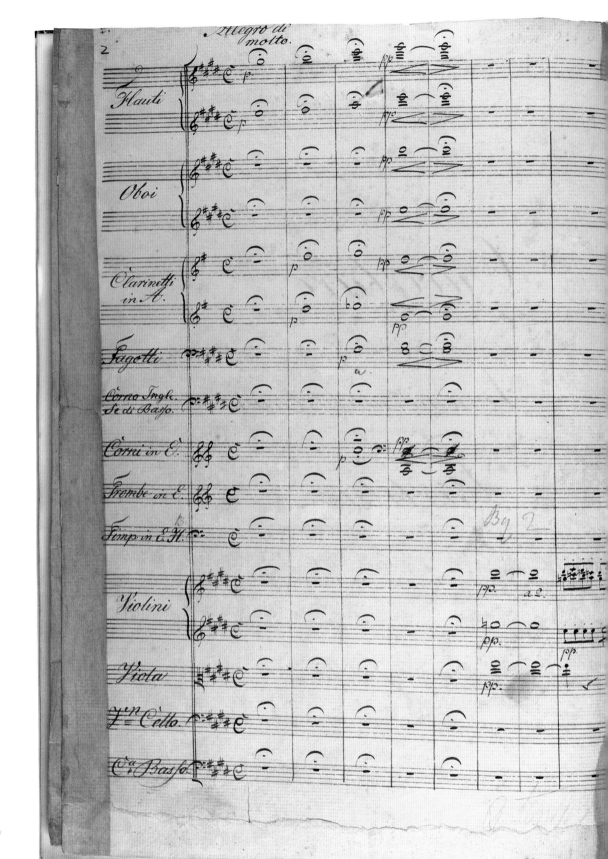

Presentation score of
*A Midsummer Night's
Dream* Overture, Op 16,
given by Felix Mendelssohn
to Sir George Smart

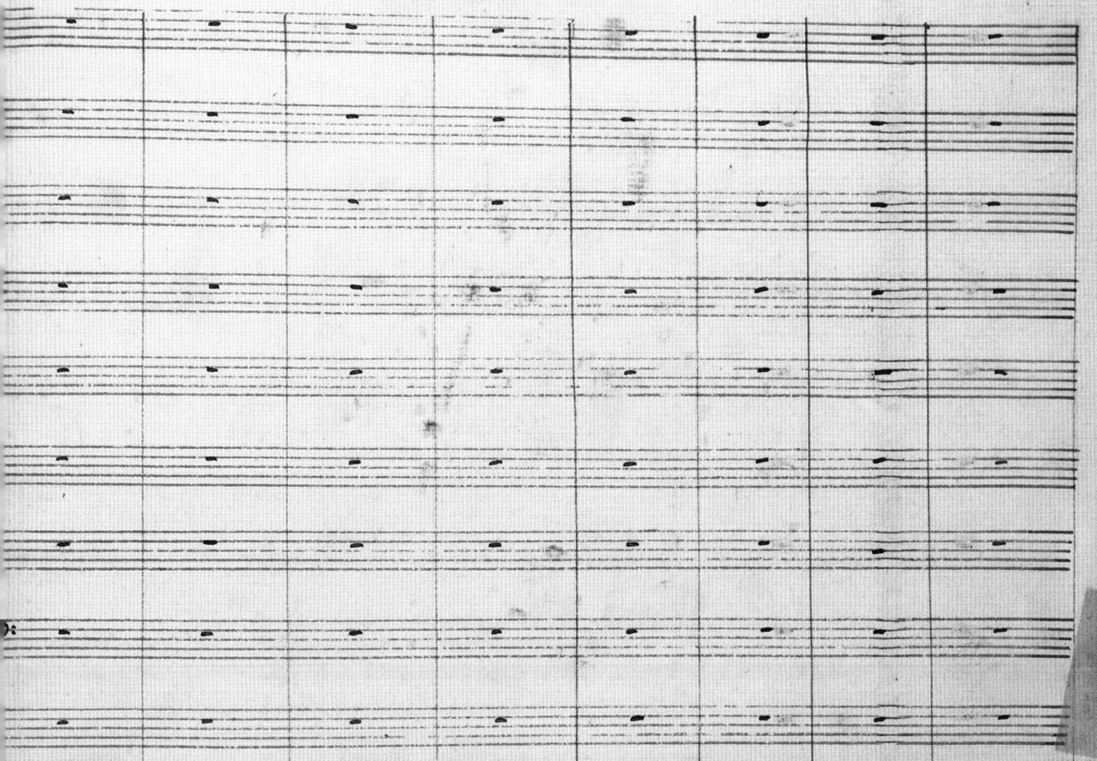
sempre staccato.
pizz.

Edward Gardner

Lucy Crowe

David Atherton and Sian Edwards, which have taken place annually since 2002. The Orchestra of the Age of Enlightenment has been a regular partner – staffed by a large proportion of alumni – for two decades and most recently there have been exciting new collaborations with the Czech Philharmonic Orchestra (inspired by their chief conductor and the Academy's Otto Klemperer Chair of Conducting, Semyon Bychkov) and an orchestral mentoring scheme with the London Philharmonic Orchestra.

Of the 500 public concerts presented each year, the Academy's annual Summer Piano Festival, founded by Head of Piano Professor Joanna MacGregor in 2014, has quickly developed into a three-day festival of cross-art collaborations. After almost a decade of immersion in Bach's choral music with the complete cantatas being performed on a Sunday lunchtime in the Duke's Hall, *Bach the European: From Ancient Cosmos towards Enlightenment* was launched in 2019 placing Bach in an

expanded, fresh and challenging new context. Looking forward to the Academy's bicentenary in 2022, major celebratory projects include the commissioning of 200 new solo works from friends and alumni of the Academy, which will build an outstanding legacy for future students and performers everywhere. This project will be expanded in local secondary schools and a series of 200 external concerts will further develop the Academy's reach.

Perhaps most striking about the Academy's distinctive character is its capacity to make it a home for so many eminent artists who regularly and generously visit to lead projects of great distinction. After the example set by Wood, Barbirolli, Mackerras and Sir Colin Davis, the Academy started to introduce a new generation of loyal conductors and versatile musicians who give time annually to students. Semyon Bychkov – whose performance of Mahler's 'Resurrection' Symphony at the Royal

Festival Hall in 2017 was widely considered one of the finest experiences of young musicians in collaboration – along with Hans Abrahamsen, John Adams, Lorenza Borrani, alumna Susan Bullock, Imogen Cooper, alumna Lucy Crowe, James Ehnes, Sir Mark Elder, alumna Catrin Finch, alumnus Edward Gardner, Richard Goode, Dave Holland, Stephen Hough, Steven Isserlis, Sir Simon Keenlyside, alumna Dame Felicity Lott, Oliver Knussen, Trevor Pinnock (the last two with whom Academy students worked in a number of exceptional recordings with its recording label, Linn), Stephen Sondheim, Christian Thielemann and Nikolaj Znaider represent a snapshot of artists who visit the Academy.

As it enters its third century, the Academy is planning to build on its global leadership in music education, dedicated to training students who through their artistry will define and shape the future of music and act as powerful advocates for its irreplaceable role in all our lives.

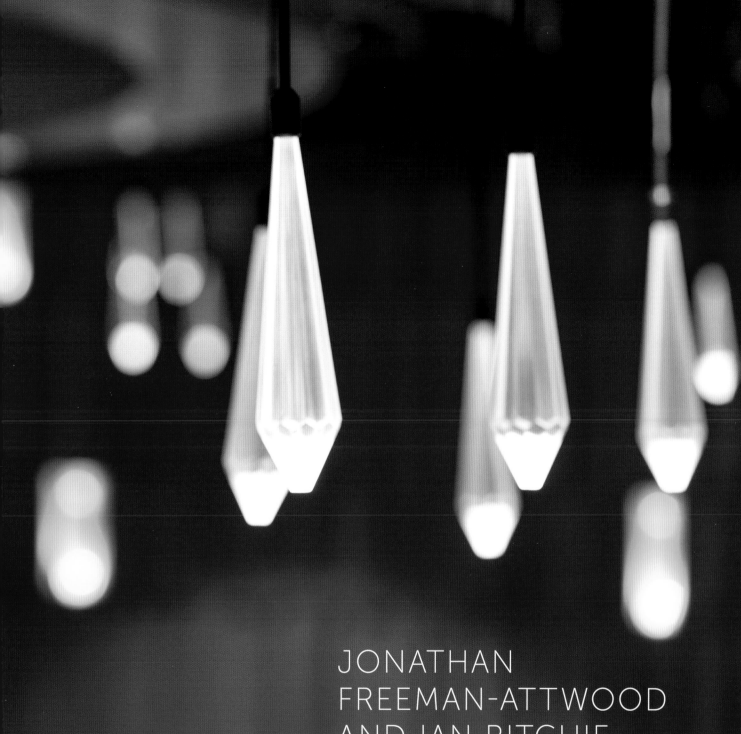

JONATHAN
FREEMAN-ATTWOOD
AND IAN RITCHIE
IN CONVERSATION

Duke's Hall,
1926

JONATHAN FREEMAN-ATTWOOD

We first met in 2009, I think. Susie Sainsbury, who had been involved in my appointment a year and a half earlier, had been encouraging me (as had other members of the Governing Body) to think as ambitiously and strategically about the next stage for the Royal Academy of Music as possible. One of the things that was becoming increasingly clear was the mismatch between the talent that was coming from all over the world and the facilities we could offer. There were a number of 'estate issues' – finding more teaching and practice space, and so on – but the most striking one was the theatre. Susie, who was part of the client team for the Courtyard Theatre you designed for the Royal Shakespeare Company and had flagged up your reputation for being able to turn very difficult projects into magical spaces, thought it would be a good idea for you to take stock of the challenge.

IAN RITCHIE

I recall anticipating some specific questions from you and immediately you said, 'Tell me about your day.' So, I thought this was a formal interview and said I'd been at Chichester Festival Theatre that morning, having stayed overnight to inspect the concrete, and that on the railway platform at 10:30 I got a phone call from an intermediary, who said, 'Are you ready to present your stadium design to Liverpool Football Club?' I said, 'Where? When?' and he said, 'Four o'clock, Mandarin Hotel, the top of Sloane Street.' Before I had finished my description of what happened, your Liverpool Football Club childhood scrapbook suddenly appeared. On the cover was Ray Clemence, the goalkeeper.

JF-A

I had actually been tipped off about our coincidental passion for the Reds (I don't usually keep football scrapbooks in Sir Henry Wood's cabinet), but it was an early indication that here was something we could explore if everything else went wrong. What I remember, very clearly, about the ensuing discussions were your *key* questions about the theatre that were absolutely fundamental to the core requirements of an ambitious conservatoire: practical issues married with the importance of creating a beautiful environment, and how it could inspire and become integral to the students' creative experience.

Opposite: Sir Jack Lyons
Theatre auditorium, 2014

'The real problem was that singers would stand and deliver but couldn't hear themselves and nor could they hear the orchestra.'

IR

I think it was about a week later that we went for a walkabout, and we were just standing on the stage of the old theatre...

JF-A

And you asked, 'if you were a twenty-one-year-old standing here, what are the problems?'

IR

A theatre is not that different from a football stadium actually. You want the emotion of being surrounded by something that brings out your best performance. Nothing worked there. The acoustics didn't feel right. The colours were awful. The lighting was pretty grim. You then produced a single A4 sheet and it was one of the best briefs I've ever received: the ambience, acoustics and intimacy, with the potential for the epic but nothing too specific for a single genre.

JF-A

The real problem was that singers would stand and deliver but couldn't hear themselves and nor could they hear the orchestra. There were aural black holes and the balance was all wrong. The fan shape was wrong too: more a conference centre layout than a creative space. The brown carpet on the walls. Yuk! The only person who ever liked it, and this shows his perverse brilliance, was Sir David Pountney when we commissioned Sir Peter Maxwell Davies's opera *Kommilitonen!* in 2010 with The Juilliard School. He walked in with the composer and said, 'This is the grungiest décor! It's perfect!'

Early visualisation by the architects showing the view from the stage in the Susie Sainsbury Theatre

IR

The first feasibility study looked at what would be a quick hit to improve the place for maybe £3 million. We might reorganise a few things and even introduce elements like a fly tower, increase the seating and see what all the ingredients would add up to. It was inevitable that once we started to consider what could be done, we soon thought about acoustics, lighting and technology, and how to optimise the circulation of people coming in and out of the theatre, and then how these improvements married up with the rest of the building. So the projected cost soon rose towards £7 or £8 million. Then we did a second feasibility study and there was a very nice moment when we found a way to achieve additional circulation. What was special was that discussions were regular and always one-to-one, and that's very rare with clients. You said to your Academic Board, 'Look, we know about music, they know about space.'

JF-A

Ever since I can remember, I'd always been told, 'You can't build a theatre. Don't touch it. It frankly isn't possible. It's a health and safety hazard. It's too expensive. You will never get planning permission.' So to find an optimist, an architect optimist who'd worked on some theatres and was not afraid of taking on the challenge, was essential.

I think, also, there's a little bit in all of us whereby if someone says you can't do something, you think 'Oh, really, can't we? Okay, we'll see about that.'

IR

It was an interesting process, because when we did the second feasibility study, introducing the circulation, there was a whole raft of questions that started to move the project into the 'transformation' bracket. It was then that we raised the possibility of building something on the roof. We got a long marked red and white pole and went up on the roof and moved it around while I wandered through the streets near Regent's Park trying to see it. We concluded that we could build an additional 6 metres up there, which nobody would really see. The question was, what could you best do with that extra space?

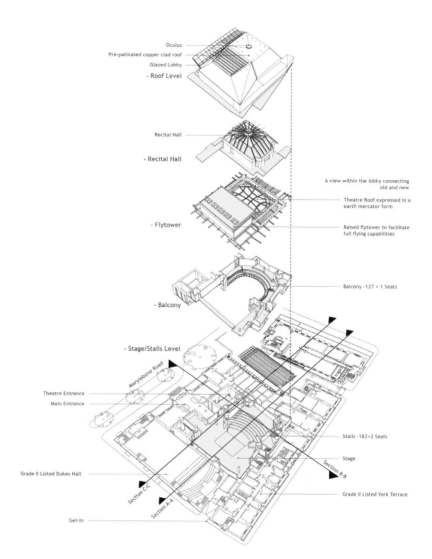

Oculus
Pre-patinated copper clad roof
Glazed Lobby
- Roof Level

Recital Hall
- Recital Hall

A view within the lobby connecting old and new

Theatre Roof expressed in a earth mercator form

Raised flytower to facilitate full flying capabilities

- Flytower

Balcony -127 + 1 Seats

- Balcony

- Stage/Stalls Level

Marylebone Road

Theatre Entrance

Main Entrance

Stalls -182+2 Seats

Stage

Section B-B

Grade II Listed Dukes Hall

Grade II Listed York Terrace

Section C-C

Section A-A

Get-In

Right: An axonometric view showing the vertical arrangement of the spaces

Below left: New light wells reveal the previously concealed Grade II-listed rear façade

Below right: East–West section showing the relationship between the Susie Sainsbury Theatre and the Angela Burgess Recital Hall above

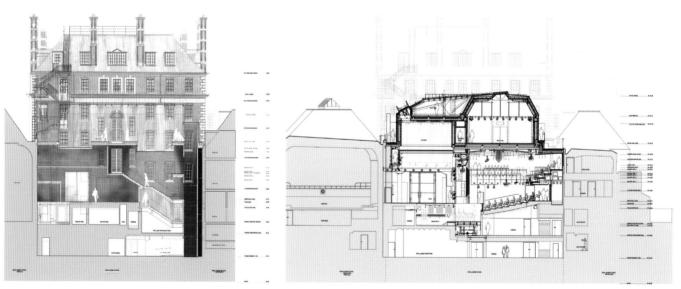

ROYAL ACADEMY OF MUSIC

O for Opera
O as sound,
of silent mouth
reflecting a surprised mind.
A symbol of wholeness,
of turning point,
and communication
which, when refined
and refined,
becomes the mind's
musical instrument.

Air pushed through
Larynx, pharynx,
oral cavity and mouth,
and most subtly shaped lips.
As sounds expand
into the rich volumed
new instrument,
a timbre floats,
wondrously alive.

Green edged roof
Of silent air
Reciting and practising,
in daylit solitude.

© 2011 Ian Ritchie

Above: Ian Ritchie's
first etching for the Susie
Sainsbury Theatre, which
envisaged a landscaped roof

Opposite: The architects'
research included exploring
the chambers and mechanics
of the human voice

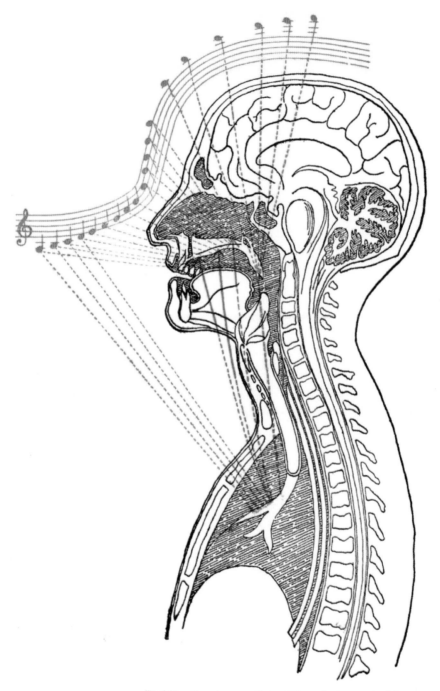

Red line denotes vocal sensation of soprano and tenor.

JF-A

Originally, the view from the park (looking towards the back of the Academy) revealed a little bit of the theatre plant room and then to the right you had nothing, just air. That's now the Angela Burgess Recital Hall. I was especially excited because we had just done a very effective piece of work filling in the adjacent nebular space – unglamorously called 'the void' – between the library and the back of the theatre to provide practice rooms and an opera studio. What is always the biggest challenge for a conservatoire is that you need lots of different kinds of spaces and there is a logjam of priorities: specialist sprung floors for Musical Theatre, orchestral rehearsal spaces, places where you can record, places for editing, reading and composing. What we had here was a chance to think a bit out of the box. So we stretched the limits and conceived the idea of another largish ensemble space, but a versatile one for public events and yet soundproofed to the extent that it could be used as a professional recording studio. It has the feel of a hovering chamber in the sky, something of a private chapel!

IR

That came from you. We had this epiphany conversation: 'Do you want practice rooms? Do you want this? Do you want that?' In the end, I said, 'Well, it might be good to have a nice space', and you said, 'That's what we need: a recital hall and recording studio in one.' And I immediately thought of a high room filled with natural light as well as music.

Every human being relates to light. If the light feels good, you feel good. That's automatic. Light is the first material of architecture. You always think, how do you bring light in? Even in the theatre where you can't have natural light, we took it into another dimension, like the night sky. The quality of light, air, sound … the silent things that you can't see. They are the first ingredients that we sense.

Opposite: The roof over the
stage of the Sir Jack Lyons
Theatre, 2014

Opposite below:
The Angela Burgess
Recital Hall is hardly visible
from the surrounding streets

Right: View over the 'strings'
of the glazed canopy at sunset

Below: The Angela Burgess
Recital Hall within its
listed-building setting,
clad in blue-grey pre-
patinated copper

JF-A

One of the things I observed after we decided how we wanted to proceed was that you would just come in and walk around the building without any obvious reason. I'd wonder why you were standing in one place for an hour or why you were moving around all those Dickensian nooks and crannies. Now I get it, at last! You were trying to find coherence between the higgledy-piggledy aspects of a building that comprises Edwardian, late Victorian, early twentieth-century and 1970s' designs and bring it all together in a kind of elusive consonance – making sense not just of the practical and navigational challenges but also the way in which aesthetically it could reflect the ethos of the institution. This is what transpires when the wonderful jewel box that is the Elton John organ kicks off against the opulent upholstering of the Duke's Hall. I love that it is an emblem of what the Academy 'does': it's got this history and rolling sense of steady sustainability, but needs to keep responding to the challenges of today. So, your ideas for the open glass in the foyer, the curve and colour of the wood – all those elements created a wonderful feeling of balance between the existing building and what it could yet become.

IR

Once we had decided that that was what we were going to do, we wrote a tougher brief. Then we produced a dossier and met the St Marylebone Society, the Marylebone Association, the Crown Estates Paving Commission, the St Marylebone Educational Trust Foundation and Savills, who were the new advisors to the Crown Estate. The De Walden Estate and the Crown Estate are the Academy's landlords, and their boundary goes right through the theatre! If you imagine the labyrinthine system of interested parties and trying to begin the project on time, it's obvious this was a huge challenge. And we were also trying to ensure planning permission that integrated full disabled access. Once you have planning permission, you have three years to find the money, so the clock started ticking and we were fundraising in a period of austerity. The banks had collapsed.

Above: View of the original 1911 main staircase from below

Left: New door openings on the main staircase provide access to the Susie Sainsbury Theatre balcony and the Angela Burgess Recital Hall above

The glazed lobby to the
Angela Burgess Recital Hall
enhances the Academy's
circulation routes, creating
a link between the old and
new buildings

JF-A

But what fortune and generosity emerged. Four members of the Governing Body immediately committed a million pounds-plus each. For the first time ever in the history of the Higher Education Funding Council of England there were no capital grants. There was absolutely no chance there, so we ended up having to do this without public money. It was all raised through private donors and trusts.

IR

If we go back to the design, we started with violins. The Project Architect José used to be in the Asociación Suzuki de Violín de Puerto Rico. He told me that they rehearsed at what used to be the residence of Spanish cellist/composer Pablo Casals. Under a rug, the current owner of the house safeguarded the floor markings created by the end pin of Casals's cello. These marks were a living memory of Casals and gave the place an uplifting aura that inspired all of the young violinists. I was convinced we needed a brilliant joinery company from whom we would learn about the varnishes, textures and surfaces that are fundamental to the acoustics. We always returned to musical instruments, whether it was the tuning of them or a series of photographs I found of the insides of stringed instruments. They were like architectural spaces. They were fabulous. If you look inside, the light is coming through and it's unbelievable.

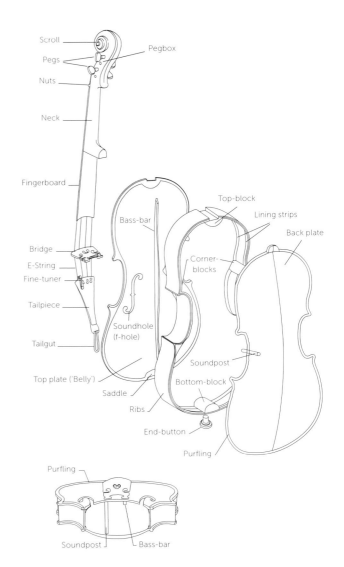

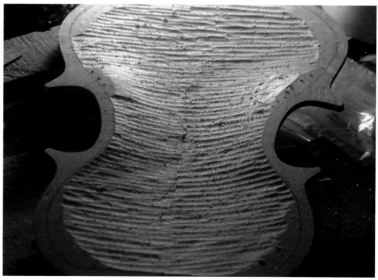

Above and opposite:
The architects' research
included exploring the
anatomy of stringed
instruments, and how
the wood is shaped
and formed

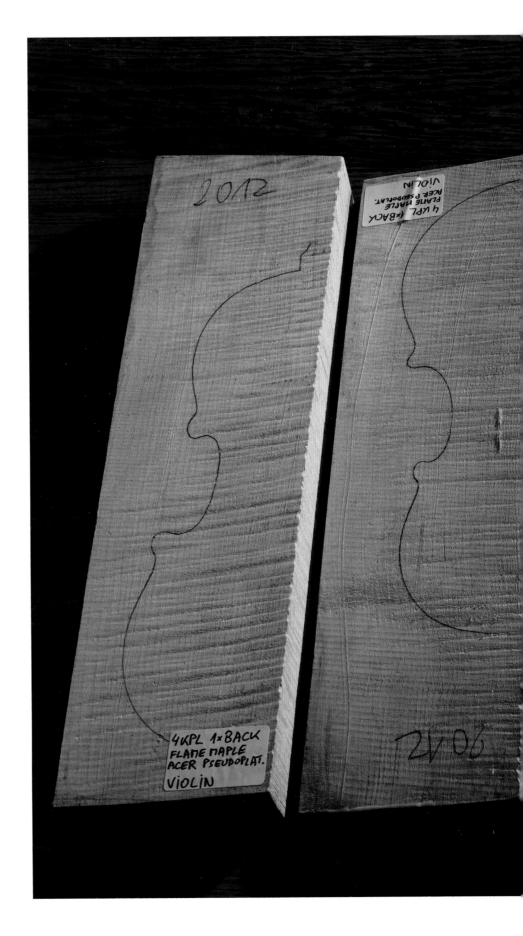

The architects researched the material characteristics of the tonewood used to create the finest stringed instruments

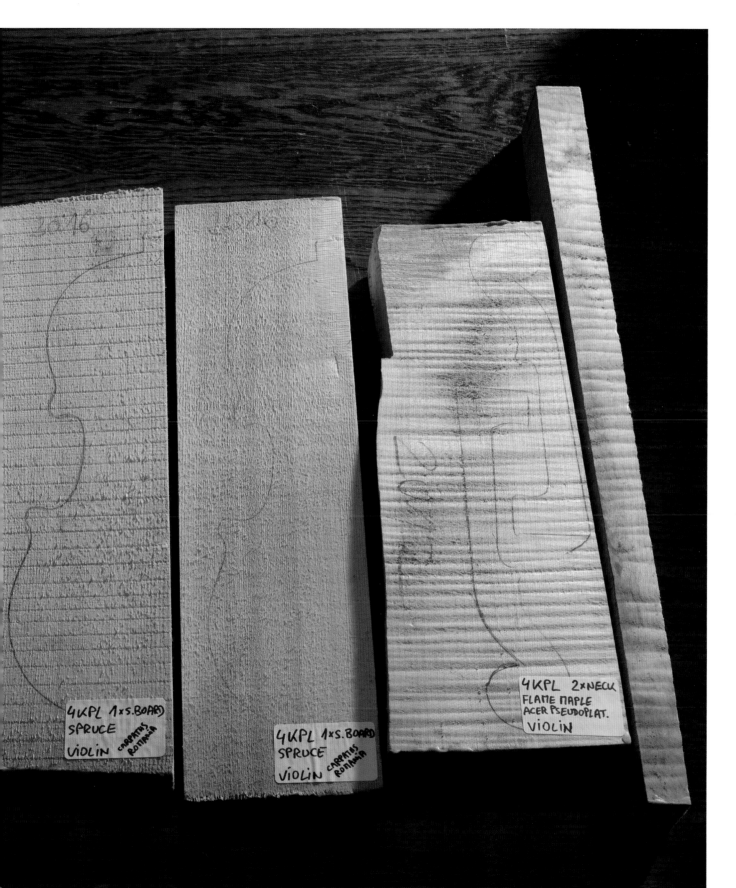

4KPL 1×S.BOARD
SPRUCE
VIOLIN CARPATUS ROMANIA

4KPL 1×S.BOARD
SPRUCE
VIOLIN CARPATUS ROMANIA

4KPL 2×NECK
FLAME MAPLE
ACER PSEUDOPLAT.
VIOLIN

'We always returned
to musical instruments,
whether it was the
tuning of them or a
series of photographs
I found of the insides
of stringed instruments.
They were like
architectural spaces.
They were fabulous.'

The architectural spaces within
stringed instruments provided
inspiration for the interior of
the Susie Sainsbury Theatre

The architects' research
included exploring the
role of varnish in
Cremona instruments

JF-A

We then went down the road to Arup, the famous acousticians, and sat in their 4D studio imagining particular kinds of music in a new space, because one key point was that we weren't just thinking about an opera theatre but also Musical Theatre, jazz and all kinds of music and ensembles.

IR

That's right. You and Susie were sitting there soaking it all up – as La Scala was being recreated by the technicians – and I was thinking two things: we're trying to design this space for listening to opera but we've also got Musical Theatre, which requires amplified sound. Philip and Ed, the acousticians, were approachable about the kind of conversations one needs to have as an architect. By using wood, you can tune the hardness and also adjust the reflection and the diffusion of sound because you can start

scratching lines in it. Knowing the basic rules, you can achieve 80 to 90 per cent of your acoustic goals right there. Conversations with Arup would normally go like this: 'We will need variable-depth big panels at the back of the auditorium'. We would say: 'Perhaps not, as there is a scale to this theatre and it must have intimacy and we have ideas for how we could achieve it. We haven't evolved them yet but we don't want things out of scale with the flowing surfaces of the space.'

JF-A

Apart from record-producing experience, this was new territory for me. I was in awe of all the expertise around the dark art of acoustics. But central to everything – design and acoustics – was our shared ideal and ambition that a successful theatre is a place where, as a performer and listener, you can go into another world, be taken out of

Above and opposite:
Full-scale prototypes
of the wall panelling were
fabricated and tested in
an acoustic laboratory
to ensure the desired
acoustic performance

Left: Susie Sainsbury,
Jonathan Freeman-Attwood
and Ian Ritchie listening to
soundscapes at the Arup
Acoustics SoundLab, 2011

Overleaf: 'Royal Academy
of Music – Opera Theatre
and Recital Hall Ceiling
Plans overlaid', a print by
Ian Ritchie Architects Ltd

yourself and your humdrum life, open yourself up, lay yourself bare to what is being presented. On top of this, it had to offer young singers and instrumentalists an environment where they could feel confident of connecting directly with their audiences, and forging their characters expressively and honestly. The nature of the cherry wood, and the added smooth and serrated lines, has created the most extraordinary warmth, and no one has to struggle to project their music. Having a hydraulic pit, the height of which can be altered, means that the balance between instruments and voices can be calibrated to fit anything from a Monteverdi opera to a contemporary show with electronics. And let's not forget also – casting one's mind back to the shortcomings of the old theatre – that we now have fantastic lighting, superb rigging, glorious winches and sensational recording facilities and video that allow us to offer professional films, edited productions and all kind of virtual presentations. The whole place is a fantastic resource for all different types of media.

IR

On the matter of experience, it really helps not having gangways and no verticality. Verticality is the killer that you often see in auditoria, music halls and concert halls. Visually, an auditorium is most often a series of horizontal curved layers and nothing jars more than introducing vertical elements such as the large undulating acoustic panels seen so commonly around the rear walls of the space.

'A successful theatre is a place where you can go into another world, be taken out of yourself and your humdrum life, open yourself up, lay yourself bare to what is being presented.'

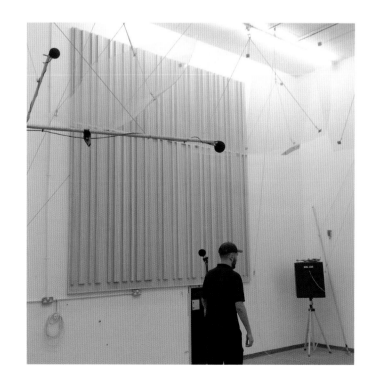

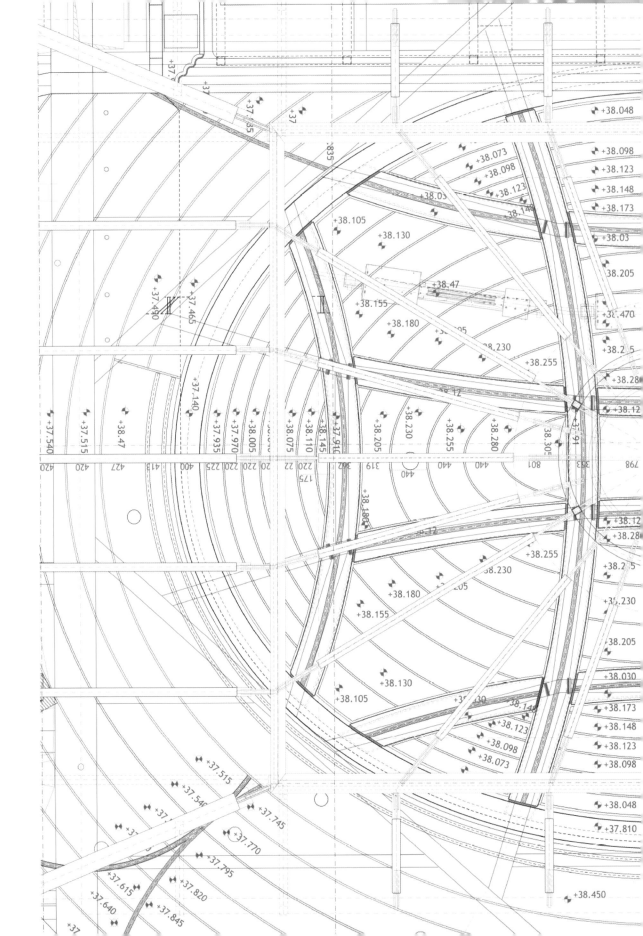

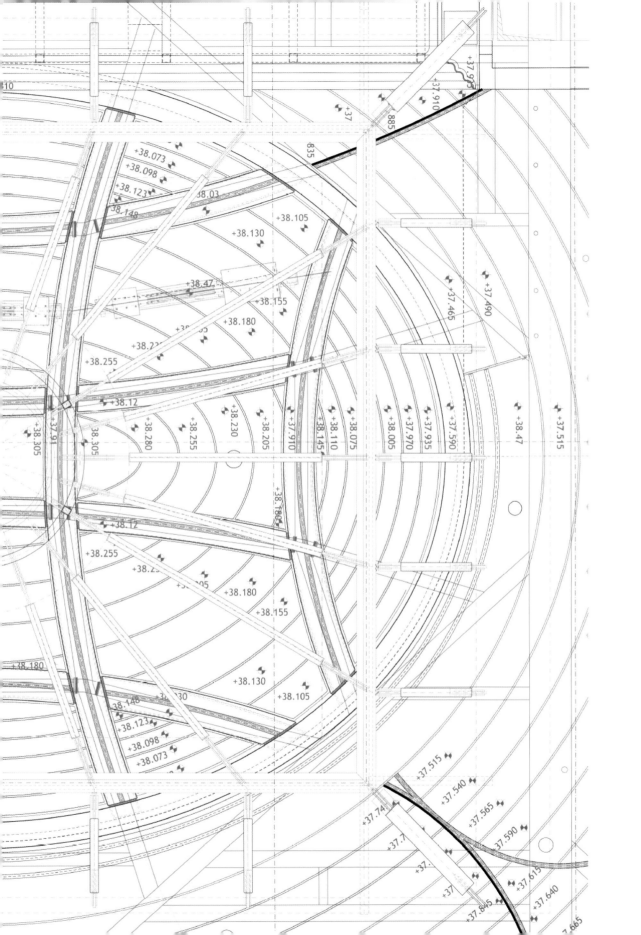

Come on, it's about time for you to tell us much more about what stimulated the overall design and structure.

In my mind's eye I envisaged a total environment – spatially, acoustically, visually warm, expansive yet intimate, exploiting lighting in a way that captured time and distance – from reading by candlelight to dreaming of the stars in the cosmos. Hence the notion of a 'Mercator'-shaped ceiling with an exploded chandelier, using fibre optics to illuminate hundreds of crystals (stars) in the ceiling, and half-crystals (candles) embedded in a 'library-like' wall lining the auditorium. The red and cream warmth of architect Frank Matcham, of Hackney Empire fame, came to mind, and that's where the vision shifted towards the red end of the spectrum: with the cherry wood being dramatised by our particular choice of red for the seats, which was inspired by the colour of Liverpool's football shirts of the 1985–6 double-winning season!

Opposite above:
The foyer of the Susie
Sainsbury Theatre

Opposite below:
Susie Sainsbury Theatre,
view from the balcony

Above: The lighting
deconstructs the traditional
chandelier into an exploding
theatre-wide galaxy of light
through 600 fibre-optic-lit
crystals

Right: The red hue of the
seating was inspired by the
Principal and architect's shared
love of Liverpool Football Club

Above left: Some crystals from the 'exploded' chandelier are embedded within the wall linings: a reference to the early days of theatre when they were lit by candlelight. The crystals provide a soft glow, each one illuminated with a miniature LED, 20 mm in diameter, designed specifically for the project

Above right: The ceiling crystals forming the 'exploded' chandelier are suspended from individual fibre-optic cables, fed by 52 LED projectors in two lighting risers accessible at balcony level

An oculus floods the Angela Burgess Recital Hall with daylight and provides the space with a central focus

JF-A

From all those involved – the architect, the engineers, construction people, subcontractors, surveyors and project managers – I kept hearing that this was 'the most complicated project ever'. It was packed to the brim with planned and unplanned challenges, and we didn't help matters by arguing for a new hall above the theatre.

IR

By placing a recital hall above the theatre auditorium we had to reinforce three of the six retained concrete columns' foundations, and this was a particular nightmare. Further piles had to be added below the second basement level foundation pads and yet more were needed to support the loads from the new steel columns. There was only about 1.8 metres of headroom into which the mini-piling rig had to fit. It was like going caving.

Opposite: Above the Susie Sainsbury Theatre and acoustically isolated from it and all other buildings, the Angela Burgess Recital Hall is entirely lined in pale, lime-washed oak

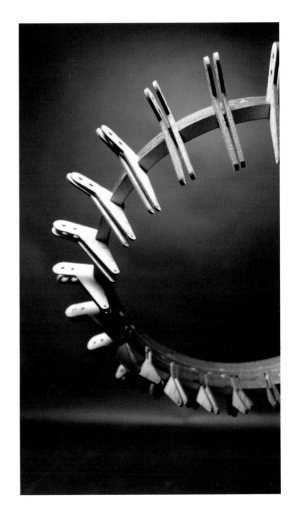

The Angela Burgess Recital Hall
roof and oculus are supported
by an expressed cable structure
invoking the image of stringed
instruments

Above left: A concept model
for the roof structure

Above right: A study
model for the oculus
'tuning' detail

Opposite: A reflected
ceiling plan

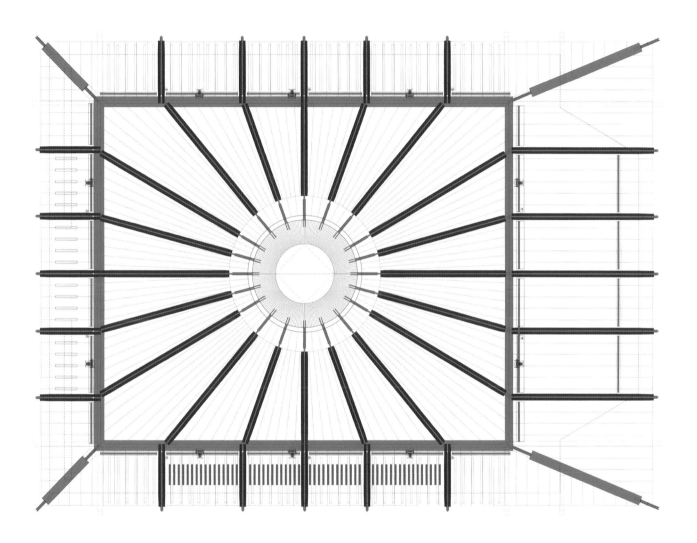

'The biggest challenge
of all was how to keep
the Royal Academy
of Music working for
two and a half years
while gutting the centre
of the building from
head to toe.'

To get a piling rig in that didn't crack into the Circle line was a challenge in itself!

However, the biggest challenge of all, from my perspective, was how to keep the Royal Academy of Music working for two and a half years while gutting the centre of the building from head to toe.

I think the complexity was compounded by the tightness of the site. There was nowhere to build. You were building inside your own building. It was like doing keyhole surgery on yourself.

And everything came in on that huge crane in the middle of the site. We had to work around the noise with a highly sophisticated timetable. The staff were all magnificent in their imagination, tolerance and teamwork.

That's right, and the construction had to be programmed around different noise levels and periods of complete shutdown to enable you to meet your educational commitments.

Opposite: A double bass
student in the Angela Burgess
Recital Hall – a naturally lit
limewashed oak-lined 'heaven'

Opposite: Above the
Susie Sainsbury Theatre,
the 100-seat Angela Burgess
Recital Hall skilfully exploits
the last major area into which
the Academy could expand,
providing 230 m^2 of additional
space for Musical Theatre,
student rehearsal, masterclasses,
performance, public events
and recording

Below left: The bow
and tuning mechanism
of stringed instruments inspired
the structural language in the
Angela Burgess Recital Hall

Below right: A detail
of the oculus structure

View of the auditorium
from stage left in the
Susie Sainsbury Theatre

JF-A

So, for example, we could teach on the third floor between
2pm and 4pm, but we couldn't do it between 4pm and 6pm,
so we had to take a lease out on six theatres (Hackney
Empire being our favourite, along with Shoreditch Town
Hall) and three major teaching buildings. There were
significant benefits. It's good for young musicians to
go elsewhere and perform to new audiences. That was
probably the best spin-off as it required a pre-professional
resourcefulness of a kind required by everybody who wants
to be a busy and active musician. If money were no object, I
would still take an opera out on tour every eighteen months.

IR

Projects like this don't come up very often in one's career,
in such a focused and exceptional environment where you
were listening to superb music-making all day long when
you came on site. Even when we were investigating what to
design, it was just gorgeous having stuff coming at you like
that. So that's very rare.

Opposite: The Susie Sainsbury
Theatre is equipped with
twenty-eight state-of-the-art
winches, with capacity for a
further seven in the future

JF-A
I would like us to highlight the sheer brilliance and beauty of the joinery.

IR
James Johnson is a company of amazing artisans who combine analogue craft with digital engineering to produce the prototypes for acoustic testing. Their skill in prefabrication was essential to achieve the quality and to overcome the construction site's spatial constraints. We also had to consider sustainability and where to source the wood. Apparently, every year there are millions of spare cherry trees in America that they don't know what to do with. Perfect! The joinery company acquired some of them.

Looking back at both spaces together, going from the cherry red warmth of the theatre to the oak whiteness of heaven in the recital hall seemed natural. The real challenge was separating them, isolating them from each other both visually and acoustically. Distance helps, obviously, and then we isolated the recital hall from the theatre, and the adjacent plant room and the glazed lobby from each other. The recital hall sits on a few hundred elastomeric bearings, which are all tuned to the correct frequencies to isolate it. So, looking up at the cosmic ceiling from within the theatre

you have no idea that there's this exquisite recital hall directly above, separated by the ceiling: a concrete slab supported on deep steel beams, and an air void within which have been placed, on a grid, all the bearings, which in turn support the precast concrete panels that support the oak timber floor of the recital hall. All quite a complex design and a tricky construction but ultimately, because of the acoustic qualities and beautiful aesthetic, hugely rewarding.

That then brings us to the whiteness and the oculus. What we did was to make sure the grain of the wood flows vertically like the light from the oculus all the way down and into the floor, and there's actually a square whirlpool in the middle. The grain of the wood and the light that's falling on the wood follow exactly the same path.

The visual rhythm of the structure comes from the tension rods, which were inspired by the strings of instruments: a cello or a violin, and bows. These references are subtle, not literal, just as the way the tension cables holding up the glass roof in the lobby follow the rhythm of the windows in the brickwork of the old building. The visual coherence is mostly subconscious to the public, but absolutely vital to the feel of the spaces.

Overleaf: The moment when the first students sang in the Susie Sainsbury Theatre

LEARNING THEIR ART
FROM THE REAL THING

Bright as sunshine on water, Holly Clark's trumpet sketches a rapid sequence of bold, angular figures, vaulting to a high C then darting down again. It is the end of the third week of Clark's first term as an undergraduate student at the Royal Academy of Music and her performance of the Toccata from Hans Werner Henze's 1974 Sonatina for solo trumpet is the opening number in a concert by the Academy Symphonic Brass under the Belgian trumpet virtuoso Jeroen Berwaerts.

Solemn and sensual sixteenth- and seventeenth-century canzons by the Venetian master Giovanni Gabrieli and an arrangement of a sonata by the Bolognese violinist Tomaso Antonio Vitali alternate with movements from Henze's Sonatina and 'Sonata per otto ottoni': baroque dances made over as abstracted cabaret, film noir and protest song. From freshers to fourth-year students there are ten trumpeters in this ensemble, seven trombonists, two tuba players and a timpanist, all of whom play a part in the virile fanfares and opulently layered chromatics of Richard Strauss's *Festmusik der Stadt Wien*, a work that zigzags between ceremonial pomp and lavish private pleasure.

Between the honeyed melancholy of *Capriccio* and the abject sorrow of *Metamorphosen*, the outrageous flourishes of the 1943 *Festmusik* sound like a blast of wilful escapism for an annexed city. To say that the work is rarely performed is an understatement: trumpet player Mark David, Head of Brass at the Academy, has played it only once in his career, with the Philharmonia Orchestra in 1991 under Giuseppe Sinopoli. Not only would the cost be prohibitive for most orchestras, but also the music is notoriously difficult to play.

Opportunities in David's department are not determined by year group but by audition, hence Clark's opening salvo. 'If I think you're good enough to do it, you do it', he says. The atmosphere as the *Festmusik* builds to its final climax – there are several – is heady. The performance is fuelled by youthful fearlessness, the sound glorious in a hall where Strauss conducted his tone poem, *Tod und Verklärung*, two years before the Anschluss.

The marquee names to have emerged from the Royal Academy of Music over the last two centuries are legendary: the conductors Sir Henry Wood, Sir John Barbirolli and Sir Simon Rattle; the horn player Dennis Brain; the pianists Dame Myra Hess, Sir Clifford Curzon and Dame Moura Lympany; the composers Sir Arthur Sullivan and Sir Harrison Birtwistle; the sopranos Dame Eva Turner and Dame Felicity Lott; the violinist Maxim Vengerov; the viola player Lionel Tertis; the singer-songwriters Annie Lennox and Sir Elton John (a former Junior Academy student and now a major benefactor). The voices in these pages are not theirs but the voices of the artists who have followed them, whose work you can hear today at the Barbican,

London; the Concertgebouw, Amsterdam; the Philharmonie, Berlin; the Walt Disney Concert Hall, Los Angeles; the Leipzig Gewandhaus; the Royal Opera House, London; the Metropolitan Opera House, New York; Wigmore Hall, London; Glyndebourne, East Sussex; and the Southbank Centre, London; in West End and Broadway theatres, in Paris, Frankfurt, Oslo, Philadelphia, Beijing and Milan; and in the fringe venues across the world where new music is sustained and reinvigorated daily. Most of them graduated from the Royal Academy of Music within a generation. Many have returned as professors or visiting professors.

They are concerto soloists, lieder and opera singers, conductors, composers, chamber musicians, early-music specialists, guitarists, organists, jazz musicians, actors, teachers, administrators and musical directors. Some of

Opposite: Bust of
Sir Henry Wood, 1936,
by Donald Gilbert,
which is used every year
at the BBC Proms and lives
in the Duke's Hall (above)
for the rest of the year

Sir Mark Elder rehearsing the
Academy Symphony Orchestra

them may be marquee names when the Academy celebrates its tercentenary. All of them play vital roles in inspiring current and future students and audiences. Their words are the glue that holds together this series of impressions from one term in the life of the Academy: observations of lessons, classes, open days, masterclasses, rehearsals, livestreamed performances and, finally, scholarship auditions, in a building that is rarely silent.

'The ensemble felt so together and secure, all that was left was to enjoy it', says trumpeter Zoë Perkins, a fourth-year undergraduate, of the Strauss. Having studied at Junior Academy, Perkins has spent much of her musical life at the Royal Academy of Music and will soon have to decide whether to continue with postgraduate studies here or elsewhere. Her predecessors in the Brass Department include Jason Evans, Principal Trumpet with the Philharmonia, and Gareth Small, Principal Trumpet with the Hallé. Together with Matthew Gee, Principal Trombone with the Royal Philharmonic Orchestra and a founder member of the Aurora Orchestra, and Martin Owen, Principal Horn with the BBC Symphony Orchestra and regular Guest Principal with the Berlin Philharmonic and the Chamber Orchestra of Europe, they are among the alumni who have returned as professors in the Brass Department.

None of them were much older than Perkins, Clark or Aaron Akugbo, first trumpet in this performance of Strauss's *Festmusik*, when they were appointed as principal players. The student routine of learning solo works and orchestral excerpts – a selection of exposed passages from core or notably challenging repertoire that is refreshed each decade – and the experience of playing in the Symphonic Brass Ensemble, the Chamber Orchestra, the Symphony Orchestra, in the pit of the Susie Sainsbury Theatre for opera or Musical Theatre productions or in the Manson Ensemble, which specialises in contemporary music, often dovetails with their first professional work. Yet every musician admits that the process of learning never stops.

'Moving excerpts from the practice room to the stage required tweaks, but no wholesale changes', says Gee. 'I'd say the biggest difference was learning to play them with a section, prioritising a more blended sound and approach. But playing first trombone also requires you to flick a switch and be able to perform more soloistically.' Owen was twenty-four and just two years out of the Academy when he joined the Royal Philharmonic Orchestra. 'If I had my time again, I would focus more on the basics', he says. 'Stop trying to run before I could walk. Listen to more concerts. Take more lessons. Prioritise learning over doing.'

As a third-year student he stepped in at short notice to play with London Sinfonietta. 'To be honest, I was struggling a little at this time, trying to piece together every aspect of technique and performance. When I got one part right, another was woefully poor. Then the Sinfonietta work came in, with a big solo horn feature. I couldn't hide or make excuses any more. It needed pure confidence and air. Just play. And that was the secret – the Holy Grail I'd been searching for. Don't think. Just play.'

Gee's first permanent job was with the Orchestra of Scottish Opera, which he combined with guest work back in London. 'I remember preparing for Sibelius's Seventh Symphony with the London Philharmonic Orchestra. I was keen to impress and wanted to play with a big, rich, dark sound, but the closer I got to the rehearsals the worse my sound got. It was sounding forced, thin, too direct and completely inappropriate for Sibelius's rich soundscape. Slightly panicked, I rushed back to London to see if one of my old teachers could offer any advice', he says.

'Within thirty seconds I was back on track. I had equated a big, rich sound with blowing more air through the trombone and physically trying force. He simply reminded me that less is more; relax the air column and get the trombone vibrating as much as possible. When I am working on sound in my own practice I still turn to this passage. It's not the famous solo, it's a little unison passage with the first trumpet, but I can immediately recall that "eureka" moment where everything clicked into place. It's one of the most useful, strongest memories I have from my studies.'

Owen recalls his first professional concerts clearly. 'I was working a lot with top orchestras. I wasn't ready. You're never ready. Not at first. But that doesn't mean you shouldn't try to do everything you can to produce the best results. I always tried to play horn solos as true solos – to come out of the texture and lead from the back – which is very different to playing them in a practice room. You have to project so much more, and often dynamics are irrelevant. Combining this with learning how to use your "radar", blending and listening all the time, was a huge challenge and still is a challenge today, as it should be if you want to play your best.'

Both players now combine solo work with their orchestral and teaching duties. Gee is a member of the Septura ensemble and has recently made his fourth solo CD, of his own arrangement of Schubert's *Winterreise*, with the pianist Christopher Glynn, another alumnus and professor. 'The player I am today was hugely influenced by

'If I had my time again, I would focus more on the basics. Stop trying to run before I could walk. Listen to more concerts. Take more lessons. Prioritise learning over doing.'

String quartet rehearsal
with students and
Levon Chilingirian

the teaching I received at the Academy but I also feel there is something special in the fabric of the place that rubs off on you and shapes you as a musician', he says. 'I believe that every successful musician has an obligation to give back and pay forward what they have learned', says Owen. 'When the Academy asked me to teach there, how could I turn my back and ignore the difference this institution has made to my life? That's the thrill and the challenge.'

Tuition on period instruments is compulsory for students in the Academy Brass Department now that many conductors routinely favour the timbres of natural trumpets, horns and trombones in music by Mozart, Haydn and Beethoven. It is also increasingly popular as a second study in the Woodwind and Strings Departments. The former divide between early and modern techniques and technology has blurred creatively, with interesting results in repertoire extending to the late Romantic. The character of a portamento slide between notes in, say, a symphony by Mahler is radically different when played with no vibrato or minimal vibrato by the strings. As Sir Mark Elder points out when he is rehearsing his Berlioz programme with the Academy Symphony Orchestra, playing with vibrato should be a decision, not a default.

When students from the Royal Academy of Music and New York's Juilliard School Brass Departments collaborated on their 2017 recording of Gabrieli's canzons under the German virtuoso Reinhold Friedrich they forged what Principal Jonathan Freeman-Attwood, himself a trumpet player and the producer of the disc, described as a stylistic 'Third Way'. The distinct traditions of two conservatoires' teaching of modern brass instruments, with young North and South American, British, Chinese, French, Italian and Spanish players, were combined with historically informed tuning, decoration and phrasing in music that sings spatially. The four-part 1608 Canzon 'La Spiritata' that featured in the Symphony Brass Duke's Hall concert was one of the most intimate works on the *Venetian Extravaganza* disc, which extended from dialogues for six, seven, eight, nine and ten players to a polychoral sonata for twenty-two players, as ornate as the architecture of the city for which it was written.

Other Royal Academy of Music recordings on the Linn label include a sequence of discs inspired by Schoenberg's Society for Private Musical Performances in Vienna: Erwin Stein's arrangement of Mahler's Fourth Symphony, Schoenberg's arrangement of *Lieder eines fahrenden*

Gesellen, and Anthony Payne's arrangement of Anton Bruckner's Second Symphony, which was commissioned by Freeman-Attwood for the Royal Academy of Music Soloists Ensemble and directed by Trevor Pinnock, harpsichordist and founder of The English Concert. Then there is Stravinsky's salty vignette, *The Soldier's Tale*, played by the Manson Ensemble and conducted by the late Oliver Knussen, with composers Sir Harrison Birtwistle and Sir George Benjamin as the Soldier and the Devil. The recording closes with a tombeau by the late Sir Peter Maxwell Davies, a dedicated professor at the Academy, whose miniature for unaccompanied violin, *A Last Postcard from Sanday*, was the starting point for the 200 Pieces bicentenary commissions, a legacy project overseen by Philip Cashian, Head of Composition. Forthcoming recordings include a further disc of Stravinsky under alumna Susanna Mälkki as part of an ongoing project with The Juilliard School.

New music has been a strong element in the violinist Thomas Gould's career. As a student, he led the combined symphony orchestras of the Royal Academy of Music and The Juilliard School at the BBC Proms under Sir Colin Davis, jammed with the jazz pianist and fellow student Gwilym Simcock, and took part in a new music exchange programme with Juilliard where he met the American composer, Nico Muhly. Muhly became a regular collaborator and wrote the concerto *Seeing is Believing* (2011) for Gould to play on a six-stringed electric violin. Gould's recital recording, *Bach to Parker*, gives an impression of the breadth of his musical interests, which he sustains by balancing work as a soloist, chamber musician and orchestral leader.

Like Zoë Perkins, who describes the student work ethic as 'infectious', Gould had studied at Junior Academy and 'already felt at home' in the building when he started as an

Academy Baroque
Soloists in rehearsal

undergraduate. Versatility, he says, has been the defining trait of his work. 'Without realising it I was already learning to handle this fluency across a number of roles during my time at the Academy. Each role requires not only a different type of playing, but crucially a different type of approach and you need to bring a different side of your personality to work. The assumption that an average day for an Academy student might include an audition for a concerto prize, a chamber ensemble rehearsal and an orchestral concert in a tutti seat was just considered par for the course.'

'The most stimulating repertoire I have found is when these varying roles can be combined, for instance when playing orchestral repertoire with a chamber music mentality – very much the modus operandi of the two chamber orchestras I have been associated with, Aurora and Britten Sinfonia – or playing a concerto while directing the orchestra from the

violin and being fully involved in all aspects of the piece, not just the solo line', says Gould.

Fellow violinist Philippe Honoré, alumnus and professor, echoes his sentiments. 'That's what motivates me as a musician, to keep the interest', he says. 'I've done chamber music and I was part of a quartet, the Vellinger Quartet. I founded an ensemble, Mobius. I played in orchestras, then I was a principal with the Philharmonia, and then I did some guest leading. I worked with some composers on pieces which were written for me. What keeps me going is no routine, basically. I like the variety. Every time I've stuck to something for too long, I think, mmm, OK, now I know how it works.'

Jack Liebeck, Émile Sauret Professor of Violin, was in his early teens when he was approached by the cellist and then Royal Academy of Music Principal, Lynn Harrell, to audition for a televised masterclass. In string-playing terms he was a

Angela Burgess
Recital Hall oculus

late starter. He was also lucky. At the age of eight, he found the right teacher and made fast progress. From fourteen he had global representation with a prominent artists' agency and divided his time between the Academy and the Purcell School.

He took his only 'A' level, in Music, studying one hour per week, in a year when he had his first engagements as a concerto soloist with the London Philharmonic Orchestra, before continuing his studies as an undergraduate. Was it possible to grow up normally? 'In the music world? It's difficult', he laughs. 'A kid that, aged ten, wants to be practising six hours a day? That's not a normal kid.'

'I feel privileged in many ways, but one of the ways in which I was privileged was to find the thing I am talented at', says Liebeck. 'Roger Federer is one of the world's greatest tennis players of all time, right? I'm pretty sure that somewhere on the planet there is someone who could have been a better tennis player than him but never picked up a racket. This goes back to the whole education thing – that every kid should have a chance to play a musical instrument. But every kid should have a chance to study with a great professor as well. I was lucky from the first lesson to the last lesson. I never had a bad lesson. I was never told the wrong thing.'

Liebeck was one of the first new professors to be appointed when the cellist Jo Cole became Head of Strings

in 2010. 'It was always in me but I had to grow into myself', he says. 'You can't be a full professor aged twenty-five. I needed to go out into the world, be recognised a bit, and then come back as a teacher.' This year he has fourteen students. 'I'm sometimes teaching them the night before I do a Wigmore recital, which a lot of players wouldn't do, but I just push through and do it', he says.

The experience of teaching has become a means of refining his own thoughts about music: 'A lot of what I do is instinctive. I just do it or did it. I think now, because I'm always trying to explain why a student should be doing something and make them understand the thought process behind it, I understand why the instinct is there. I think I've gained a lot more understanding from teaching because instead of just feeling a chord progression, which I feel very deeply, in my blood, I have to start explaining why that progression is different from another progression. What works with one student doesn't work with another. That's a long process. You give them ideas in a lesson and then you try something else.'

Crisp light floods through the oculus of the Angela Burgess Recital Hall as the celebrated Canadian violinist James Ehnes listens carefully to Australian student Bridget O'Donnell playing the first movement of Mozart's Violin Concerto No. 3 in G. A few days earlier, Ehnes played a recital of Beethoven's Sonatas at Wigmore Hall. Two days before

Opposite: James Ehnes giving a violin masterclass in the David Josefowitz Recital Hall

Lorenza Borrani leading
an ensemble in the Angela
Burgess Recital Hall

Portland stone busts outside the
David Josefowitz Recital Hall

that, he was the soloist in Walton's Violin Concerto with the London Philharmonic Orchestra under the orchestra's new Chief Conductor and Academy alumnus, Edward Gardner.

O'Donnell's Mozart is period-inflected, citrus-sharp and vividly animated, quite unlike Ehnes's smoother approach. But Ehnes, who is, like Nikolaj Szeps-Znaider, one of several dozen famous visiting professors, is smiling, respectful and engaged. The intimacy and clarity of sound in this room, described by Freeman-Attwood as 'a little private chapel' on top of the Susie Sainsbury Theatre, makes it more than a performance space. It is ideally proportioned for the detailed work of a masterclass, and acoustically pristine. The first commercial recording to be made here, of the baroque violinist Rachel Podger's interpretation of Bach's Cello Suites, won a Diapason d'Or award, something that Freeman-Attwood, who produced the disc, attributes to what this room offers as a professional recording venue. But it remains primarily a place for learning.

Ehnes calmly discusses technical and interpretive details with O'Donnell, encouraging her to tighten her bow a little, to find a way to make the 'beautiful, creative and subtle things' she is doing speak to a larger space, as though she were playing in front of an orchestra. They work together on 'opening out the mechanism' of violin playing, sustaining

the audibility of a decay, and maximising the opportunities in this movement of the concerto to 'hold a note and make it beautiful'. They play with the idea of making one phrase more operatic – 'Could you be a bit more rude?' he asks the pianist – and it begins to sing. This breaking down of less than ten minutes of music into a chain of connected cells, punctuating and clarifying a musical argument, is an exercise that happens in every department, in one-to-one lessons, and in chamber and orchestral rehearsals.

Busts and portraits of musicians and benefactors line every corridor in the building. Outside the David Josefowitz Recital Hall, Portland stone busts of Beethoven, Mozart, Bach, Haydn, and a figure that is either Henry Purcell or a substantially nipped and tucked Handel are lined up, survivors of the bombing raid that destroyed the Queen's Hall, the original location for the Henry Wood Proms, in 1941. When the consort of singers for the December concert of the Bach Cantatas series rehearse, they are watched by the Hon. Cecilia Cavendish Anderson, resplendent in an ermine-trimmed opera coat, with a fan of turquoise ostrich feathers. One face in particular haunts the building, beautiful and dreadfully sad, that of Harriet Cohen, the pianist who was for many years the muse and lover of the composer Arnold Bax, and whose collection of art is concentrated in Jo Cole's office and includes a work by Marc Chagall.

Liebeck is unstinting in his praise of Cole's leadership, and credits her with much of the modernisation of the Strings Department, one of the largest in the Academy. At current count, seventy-two string alumni hold principal positions in orchestras across the globe. This figure does not include leading chamber players and players working in film studios and multimedia. As a cellist, Cole worked as a soloist, chamber musician and orchestral player, and still occasionally joins the London Symphony Orchestra when her schedule allows. She describes the three disciplines as 'the Holy Trinity' and revises her survival guide for new students every year, a document that aims to reassure any fretful parents. She is particularly proud of the emerging string quartets in the department, including O'Donnell's quartet, The Hill Quartet.

'Obviously the key thing when people come here is their principal study and their work with their teacher. But that to me is just the door opening, really. If they're spending four years here you have to get them to be as good as they can

possibly be, but that means that they have to be completely open to what those possibilities are', says Cole.

'It is a sort of mystery, really, what the music profession consists of, but freshers generally have a rather one-dimensional view that either you're a dazzling soloist or you sit in an orchestra or you teach or you're in a quartet, none of which is true. Everything is a purée of so many different elements. It's a question of not just explaining that but of exciting them, and saying that all these possibilities are open to you. I love it when they have a passion for a particular thing, whether it's early music or chamber music. That's fabulous and we ought to nurture it', she says.

'There's a moment around the fourth week of term when the penny drops that this isn't a summer music course. I'm always very interested in that moment. It's a noticeable watershed when all of their past schooling becomes less influential and they move into becoming a true student. There's a huge mix, some from specialist music schools, some from comprehensive schools, some from public and

Above: Cello student practising alongside a portrait of Henry Purcell

Right: Nikolaj Szeps-Znaider working with students in the Angela Burgess Recital Hall

Opposite: Marin Alsop rehearsing the Academy Symphony Orchestra

international schools. You see an absolute blossoming and I love that.'

Cole is refreshingly sceptical about the idea of strict adherence to certain schools of violin teaching: the Russian tradition, the schools of Émile Sauret or Leopold von Auer. 'There's a definite family tree, that's true of violins, violas and cellos as well. It's a question of how you fold that into the technique of playing. Having hard and fast rules about what category you fall into, I think it's counterproductive. It's important to take elements of different styles because of the variety and depth of music that is played now. If you pursue a very narrow path, there will be areas that will be out of bounds.'

How hard is it to balance giving technical and interpretive advice with allowing the individual musical voice of the student to be heard? 'I think the worst sort of teaching is "Do it like this"', she says. 'That's like building photocopiers. If you can get them to make their voice as clear as possible and then get them to work with the voice that they have, for me the initial stage is making sure that they do establish a voice.'

'Sometimes a student will play a long note in a Beethoven or Brahms sonata and just play the note. You have to think, what's happening? What is the piano doing? I think asking a lot of questions of them tends to reveal what they're trying to do, and then the thing is to help them do that. If the student says, "I want to make this sound really intense", then you can say, "have you tried a different contact point [of bow and string] or a faster vibrato?", and just encourage them to experiment and discover what it is they want to say.'

In Graham Mitchell's double bass masterclass, finding the contact point is everything. Of the stringed instrument family, his is the largest. 'You have to let your body weight make the sound', he tells the students, using their instruments to illustrate his points and encouraging them to vocalise the lines they have to play. 'Until the technical tools are in place it is very difficult to let your musical interpretation sing', he says. Part of that process comes down to finding the right instrument. The Academy's world-renowned collection allows for long-term lending to students but what happens when they have to hand them back?

Cole is mindful of the difference between a wonderful instrument and an expensive instrument. 'We are in a golden period of instrument making at the moment, so it's a question of breaking down the traditional resistance to newly varnished instruments and actually discovering the exceptional quality that is out there. A dealer's fine instrument isn't necessarily a player's fine instrument', she says. The same applies to bows. Her own is one that she has had since she was eleven. 'It's not valuable,' she laughs, 'except to me.'

No matter how technically advanced the students are, they are still growing up. 'As something of a late developer, between the ages of eighteen and twenty-three I was still experiencing exciting changes and discoveries away from the violin', says Thomas Gould. 'I clearly recall, aged twenty-one, my teacher György Pauk exclaiming, "What has happened to your playing? It's transformed from last week!", to which I rather sheepishly replied that I had that week acquired my first girlfriend!' Cole's handbook includes advice on dealing with stress and homesickness, diet,

laundry, time-keeping, practising, meeting expectations in recording sessions, giving and receiving constructive criticism, and even which direction to look when crossing the road – an essential for international students.

Cole experienced what she described as a kind of 'grieving process' when she took the job, cutting back her playing commitments and returning to the institution where she studied herself in the early 1980s, but it was a conscious decision to give back some of what she had been given. 'I love the students and I love the profs. They are amazing. And watching what happens here, the alchemy', she says. Her colleague Jo Knight, another cellist who returned as professor, describes the Academy as a place that has been transformed in recent years, not least to reflect the changes in the industry. 'It is certainly a highly competitive profession to currently embark on and one which is perhaps harder to crack than twenty years ago', says Knight. 'But I do feel that we prepare our students fastidiously for both on and off the stage. To have every aspect of guidance from instrumental expertise

to negotiating and planning programmes and concerts, everything is covered.'

'It's a balance between looking forward and also wanting to preserve', says Cole. 'To use tradition not as a crutch but as a springboard. That's critical. If you stagnate, it takes a long time to recover. You want to use the richness and security and knowledge and experience but every year you get new blood. And when you realise you're saying something to someone who has never heard it before, you've got to keep it fresh.'

In the Duke's Hall the violinist Lorenza Borrani, leader of the Chamber Orchestra of Europe and co-founder of the Italian orchestral collective, Spira mirabilis, is rehearsing the Academy Chamber Orchestra with the Principal Cellist of Spira mirabilis, Luise Buchberger. It is the end of their third day of an intensive week working with the students on Haydn's Overture to *L'isola disabitata* and Beethoven's Eighth Symphony, in collaboration with the horn player Francesco Bossaglia. Currently they are focusing on two small but crucial corners of the Haydn.

The section in question is in minuet form, a phrase that is repeated twice by the strings, warmed with a single flute, then reignited by the cellos, among them Sheku Kanneh-Mason, fresh from recording Elgar's Cello Concerto with Sir Simon Rattle. Although the rhythm of this passage comes from a dance, the coolness of the orchestration and the severity of the harmony are more suggestive of sacred music. With no conductor in front of them, the ensemble depends on breathing together and paying attention to each other in order to adjust articulation, dynamics and pulse as one body. 'Listen to the harmonies', says Borrani to the students, pointing to one progression. 'I wouldn't stretch that bar too much', adds Buchberger, 'We are already in G minor. It's no surprise.'

The next day's performance is exhilarating. Whatever has happened in the previous days, it is not just Borrani and Buchberger shaping the Haydn. Students Jack Greed, leader of the second violins, and Shing To Mak, Principal Bassoonist, are also pivotal to the sudden mood and tempo changes of Haydn's *Sturm und Drang* style, introducing new

Above: Philippe Herreweghe leading a Bach rehearsal

Overleaf: Rehearsal for woodwind, brass and percussion students with Mark David in the Duke's Hall

ideas and new material, navigating a complex argument. The Beethoven, too, is volatile and bold. The Allegro scherzando is ticklish with pert quavers from the woodwind and furtive, playful nudges from the cellos. The Tempo di menuetto is broad and pungent, with a Trio section of Brahmsian beauty from Buchberger, accompanied by the clarinets, bassoons and horns. There is Mendelssohnian fizz to balance the raucous propulsion of the final movement and the sudden interruption from the cellos and basses that sounds like a dry run for the finale of the Ninth Symphony.

The volume of new ideas, accents, colours and textures is dizzying, informed by the knowledge of what Beethoven wrote before the Eighth Symphony, and what he would write after it. There are hugs and handshakes between desk partners at the end of the concert. In the band room the flautists and oboists pose for selfies with Borrani. The students know that this was a remarkable performance – and not merely because they played Haydn and Beethoven with two women who have worked as principals with Claudio Abbado, Nikolaus Harnoncourt, Bernard Haitink, Yannick Nézet-Séguin, Sir Simon Rattle and Sir John Eliot Gardiner. As Borrani explains, playing without a conductor, as Spira mirabilis does, rehearsing intensively

and democratically, is 'about responsibility, listening and reacting, power and freedom.'

What did she and Buchberger mean when they spoke about surprise in the previous day's rehearsal? 'This music is old. We should not be afraid to say that', says Borrani. 'But the composers were writing to surprise. It's very hard to find someone who is surprised by the first notes of, for example, Beethoven's Fifth Symphony now, but it is there. We have to make an effort to discover it.' What would she like the students to take away from the experience of working with her? 'To try to go behind what is written. What we have is only a suggestion. If we believe in this music we have to do more, not just make a beautiful sound. We have to take risks.'

There is a huge difference between the working lives of a violinist such as Daniel Hope and a cellist such as Rachel Helleur-Simcock. Hope is a soloist, travelling constantly, whereas Helleur-Simock has made her home in the Berlin Philharmonic. As a teenager who, like Liebeck, was already performing concertos under immense pressure, Hope commuted once a month to Lübeck for his lessons with Zakhar Bron.

'I don't feel that an institution, as good as it may be, can prepare you fully for a soloist's career. That comes from

Left: Maxim Vengerov leading a masterclass in the Duke's Hall

Opposite: Murray Perahia rehearsing in the Duke's Hall

getting out on the road and sticking it out', he says. What advice would he give an aspiring soloist? 'Work hard, find your niche and remember that the re-engagement makes the career, not the initial engagement.' When he is not playing music, he is writing about it. 'It's something that Jonathan Freeman-Attwood instilled in me. It started in 1999 when I wrote the liner notes for my first album and has continued now for twenty years, culminating in four books and regular columns about music.'

Helleur-Simcock emphasises the importance of physical and mental health for the developing musician: 'Exercise, Alexander Technique and good nutrition but also self-care and being kind to yourself are necessary components of being and staying a professional musician.' Her first love was always symphonic repertoire. She recalls a lesson with Philip Sheppard, late in her years of study at the Royal Academy of Music, at a point when she was struggling with doubts about her playing.

'Philip asked what I dreamt of doing and threw out a couple of questions, one of which was "Well, would you like to be in the Berlin Phil?" I laughed out loud but something in his expression made me realise he wasn't joking. Obviously he couldn't have known then if I actually had a chance or not of getting into that orchestra, but just the fact that it didn't seem outside the realms of possibility felt like a whole new world to me.'

As a student Helleur-Simcock took part in the London Symphony Orchestra String Experience Scheme and did a trial with the BBC Philharmonic. She then took further studies at the Hochschule für Musik 'Hanns Eisler' in Berlin and was accepted into the Karajan Akademie of the Berlin Philharmonic, taking individual lessons and receiving chamber music coaching while rehearsing and performing with the orchestra. Her first job was as Principal Cellist of the Deutsche Oper, Berlin – 'a baptism of fire in terms of the repertoire and doing it all in a foreign language' – before she joined the Berlin Philharmonic itself. Cellists Louisa Tuck and Alberto Casadei have followed similar paths as principals with the Oslo and Rotterdam Philharmonic Orchestras, as have double bassists Dominic Seldis and Felix Lashmar with the Royal Concertgebouw Orchestra.

'It's hard to generalise about differences between UK and German orchestras because all orchestras are unique

and have their own cultures', Helleur-Simcock says. 'I suspect my orchestra may be one of the most "unique" of them all. The Berlin Philharmonic is made up of a collective of such strong players, with such strong ideas and egos. I'm lucky that the orchestra isn't on the road quite as much as some others, although it's still quite a lot. I do find it tiring when the tours are especially long, but of course it's always fun to see new places, although you never have as much time there as one would think. I just try to enjoy the times at home with my husband as much as possible, as it's never long before one of us has to hit the road again!'

Forty-eight hours before the 2019 Autumn Piano Festival, *Politics and Protest*, a video goes viral on social media. In the third week of civil unrest and state reprisals in Chile, an orchestra and chorus are performing 'El pueblo unido, jamás será vencido' in the streets of Santiago amid a crowd of citizens protesting against the government of Sebastián Piñera. Other videos have already circulated from Santiago, among them soprano Ayleen Jovita Romero singing 'El derecho de vivir en Paz' from her window after curfew, but 'El pueblo unido', written before General Pinochet's 1973 coup, is the song on which the American composer Frederic Rzewski's 1975 piano work *The People United Will Never Be Defeated!* is based.

Performed in relay in the Angela Burgess Recital Hall by students George Fu, Julian Chan, Mihaly Berecz and Harry Rylance, Rzewski's variations bite and splash and dazzle. There are deep, plummy, secretive chords that seem to have been plucked from Clara Schumann or Johannes Brahms, tongue-in-cheek flurries of Rachmaninovian virtuosity, improvised shouts, gasps and whistles from the players. There are stylistic, colouristic or melodic allusions to Purcell, Debussy, boogie-woogie, blues, spirituals and national anthems, packaged up with Beethovenian ambition and disruptive wit.

Students performing in
the Summer Piano Festival

Sir Harrison Birtwistle
rehearsing the Academy
Manson Ensemble

It is a technical tour de force, with one pianist holding a chord as another slides into his place at the piano stool, a statement and a provocation that ends, in this performance, with all four pianists playing a reprise of the song together. It is also a work that would likely have been considered unplayable, or at least undesirable, in a conservatoire context twenty years ago.

Head of Piano, Professor Joanna MacGregor, resists the idea that she has revolutionised the repertoire played at the Academy, pointing out that one of the first things she did on her appointment was to introduce exams in Mozart and Beethoven Piano Concertos. But today's four-concert marathon of music from Liszt transcriptions to improvisations on texts by Bertolt Brecht, via works by Leoš Janáček, Fazıl Say, Nikolai Medtner, György Ligeti, Anton Webern, George Crumb and Mozart, illustrates the inquisitiveness she inspires in her pupils.

The department has always favoured individuality, as demonstrated in the diversity of repertoire of alumni Christian Blackshaw, Gabriela Montero, Yevgeny Sudbin,

Inon Barnatan, Karim Said, Kit Armstrong, Freddy Kempf and Benjamin Grosvenor, and the acclaimed lieder accompanists, Graham Johnson and Iain Burnside. MacGregor has added to the curriculum classes in early keyboards, conducting from the keyboard, curating programmes, playing to silent films and working with actors.

'I think if you're a pianist you're rather lucky, because playing the piano implies a lot of versatility anyway', she says. 'You've got this huge solo repertoire to choose from but inevitably you're also going to be doing a lot of accompanying and a lot of chamber music. And then it doesn't take very far to nudge them towards improvising. So, for example, as part of this Mozart Piano Concerto exam for third-year undergraduates, there are prizes for writing or improvising your own cadenza. You can't just learn Clara Schumann's cadenza. You must write your own.'

MacGregor insists on close examination of a complete orchestral score, whether the work is a piano concerto or, as today, one of Liszt's transcriptions of a Beethoven

Opposite: Professor Joanna MacGregor teaching a one-to-one lesson

symphony. She says that her students are hungry to learn and experiment, and that jazz classes can enlighten a player's approach to Bach's French Suites. There have been inevitable battles with the piano technician over works for prepared pianos, such as John Cage's Sonatas and Interludes, but 'they all love it and they want to do it. They come here at eighteen, a lot of them, and when they're that young they're just so open. They're just so excited and quick. They don't have barriers.'

'Most of them have come here to become a performer, and they may well discover when they're here that they're going to be composers, say, or chamber musicians, but they come initially because they think they're going to be solo performers', say MacGregor.

'Being a solo performer is quite tough. It involves a lot of things which aren't just about the playing. It involves the ability to have a heavy workload, to learn pieces quickly, to not get tired, to be able to travel, to know how you react on the day of a concert, how to deal with nerves, how to look after yourself physically, eating, sleeping, how to build up your stamina, because there's lots of stamina involved when you're a pianist. One-to-one lessons are for this very intimate, close collaboration with your teacher, musically and technically getting under the bonnet of a piece and learning how to play things, developing over a number of years. But of course you then have to get up on stage and see what happens.'

Kit Armstrong is a case in point: a former child prodigy (a term he refuses to see negatively), Armstrong studied Natural Sciences and Pure Mathematics and combines his career as a pianist with composing. The academic side of his studies at the Academy was what he found most influential on his music-making in the long term, especially music history. 'I often dedicate piano recitals to the works

of the English virginalists, and I am currently composing an opera on Guillaume de Machaut', he says.

Karim Said, who left Jordan to study in the UK at the age of eleven, remembers his teacher Tatiana Sarkissova as 'the most dedicated and inspiring of teachers' but points, too, to the impact of a visit to the Academy by the conductor Sir John Eliot Gardiner. 'I remember being struck by the fact that he openly disliked Wagner', says Said. 'I'd never heard a musician being so explicitly anti any particular composer, but learned quickly that it must have been everything that Wagner stood for in Gardiner's eyes, as well as his music, that he apparently hated. That got me thinking, even as a huge Wagner fan. One of the pieces on the programme he conducted was Monteverdi's *Lamento della Ninfa*. This performance is embedded in my musical memory as my first real introduction to Monteverdi, whom I'm now passionate about as a composer who is central to musical awareness.'

Both pianists are cautious about the idea of aiming to be a 'professional soloist'. Armstrong believes in 'education for education's sake'. Said says that he does not consider himself to be a soloist in the traditional mould. 'I'm rather excited about the way that my career continues to develop in quite a few tangents simultaneously. I do not tour the world's largest concert halls playing different piano concertos with top orchestras, even though that was once a dream.'

'I couldn't have imagined that I would direct a chamber orchestra with its own concert series as one of its founders in my native Jordan, in the same year as the release of my second album, playing Byrd and Schoenberg on the modern piano, while playing concerts as part of the Boulez Ensemble in Berlin, my current city of residence, under Daniel Barenboim.' He traces his range of interests back to the Academy, warning that the 'single-track model' works for only a tiny minority of musicians.

Percussion Showcase
rehearsal in the Duke's Hall

Fritz Schönpflug's 1907 cartoon of Mahler slumped in front of a cowbell, rute and hammer captures a watershed moment in the history of orchestral percussion. The punchline reads, 'My god, I forgot the car horn! Now I will have to write another symphony!' From Mahler's Sixth Symphony (timpani, bass drum, snare drum, cymbals, triangle, cowbells, hammer, tam tam, rute, bells, glockenspiel and xylophone) to Edgard Varèse's 1926 modernist riverscape *Amériques* (most of the above in multiples plus ratchet, sleigh bells, lion's roar, whip, slapsticks, gongs, castanets, sirens, wind machine and boat whistle), the range of sounds from sinister to comical, and from industrial to rural, required from a percussion section grew exponentially.

Take the side drum out of Ravel's *Boléro* or the first movement of Shostakovich's *Leningrad Symphony* and you take the engine out of the car. Remove the timpani from Brahms's First Symphony and you lose the depth of tone, seriousness and joy. From the kettledrums in Purcell's *Funeral Music for Queen Mary* to the Jingling Johnny or Chapeau Chinois in Lully's 'Marche pour la cérémonie des Turcs' and Beethoven's Ninth, and the unsettling sound of

stone knocked against stone in Brett Dean's opera, *Hamlet*, percussion can add colour, character or punctuation.

In Gerald Barry's *The Importance of Being Earnest* forty plates are smashed in succession. In Academy alumnus Philip Venables's *4.48 Psychosis* the psychiatrist's voice is represented by the rumble of drums in speech rhythms. Metal, wood and skin are the materials that propel the great percussion ensemble works of the 1970s: Steve Reich's *Drumming* and Iannis Xenakis's *Pléïades*.

Alumnus Sam Walton can often be seen playing alongside the Head of Percussion, Neil Percy, in the London Symphony Orchestra, and in the London Philharmonic Orchestra, London Sinfonietta and the Chamber Orchestra of Europe. Alumnus and visiting professor Colin Currie works as a concerto soloist, in a duo with Walton, and as founder of the Colin Currie Group, playing works such as Reich's *Drumming*.

Currie has given premieres of works by Muhly, Louis Andriessen and Anna Clyne, but the alumna who has done most to bring percussion to the front of the stage, as performer and commissioner of new music, is Dame Evelyn Glennie. She was the first deaf student to be admitted to the

Opposite: Oliver Knussen rehearsing
the Academy Symphony Orchestra,
view from the percussion section

Academy, the first percussion student to give a solo recital there, and the first to play a percussion concerto there, collaborating with composer and fellow student, Kenneth Dempster, in the early 1980s.

Battling an institutional focus on orchestral percussion, Glennie 'delved into baroque repertoire and indeed anything I could tackle and was convinced would work on percussion' as a student, and 'spent many an hour playing in corridors, empty toilets, any space I could find in order to make the musical decisions on my own'. Her greatest influence at this point was James Blades, the percussionist who had premiered many of Britten's works and visited the Academy every term.

'This was always such a joyous and exciting time. Through James I realised what it meant to be a musician and how it can truly affect others. He was such a great communicator both through musical language and the spoken word; everything was a discovery for him; he had a way to make everyone he met feel special and interesting. The sessions I had with James really influenced me far deeper than being a percussionist or musician. He helped me to better understand about sound and how it can affect us. I very much treasured our time together, so much so that I kept in touch with him until his death at the age of ninety-seven. There is hardly a day that goes by without my thinking of James.'

During the Timpani and Percussion Department's Open Day Neil Percy leads a tour of the studios. There are students playing delicate arrangements of Bach keyboard miniatures on marimba and dazzling vibraphone improvisations

Percussion student practising
in the Duke's Hall

'You can't play
with your whole
soul if your body
isn't part of that.
If you play with your
whole being it's
completely different.'

on Jimmy McHugh's 1930 song, 'On the Sunny Side of the Street'. They are expected to have range: percussion student Andrea Domínguez de Dios will play works by the Academy's Oliver Knussen Chair of Composition, Hans Abrahamsen, with the Manson Ensemble this term and works by Stephen Sondheim and Leonard Bernstein in the pit for the Musical Theatre Department's showcase.

A workshop on Basel drumming sees a group of piccolo players dissolving into giggles. During the Latin American percussion session led by recent alumnus Jake Brown and Academy Fellow Matthew Farthing, the youngest and quietest visitor, still in her school uniform and accompanied by her parents, suddenly blossoms, leading the twelve-strong group of drummers and shakers with verve and sass to match the pithy chime of the agogo bells.

Tom Greenleaves knew that he wanted to be a timpanist at the age of twelve. He is now Principal Timpanist of the Leipzig Gewandhaus and describes it as his 'dream job'. As a boy he was obsessed by symphonic repertoire, then, when he was fourteen, the BBC chose 'Nessun dorma' as the theme music for its coverage of the 1990 World Cup. The first classical CD he bought with his own money was Zubin Mehta's recording of *Turandot* with the London Philharmonic Orchestra and Luciano Pavarotti. 'That was what opened up the world of opera', he says. Sir John Eliot Gardiner's Bach recordings were another early touchstone, as was Brahms. Approximately half of Greenleaves's work in Leipzig is opera. He also regularly deputises at the Bayerische Staatsoper in Munich, under conductors such as Kirill Petrenko, and plays Bach with the Gewandhausorchester in Leipzig's Thomaskirche.

What was the first time in the Thomaskirche like? 'Unbelievable', he says. 'Because you know that it's Bach's church. He's buried there up in the chancel and it's always packed out. He's lying there and the choir you perform with, well, now it's 808 years old, and it's just indescribable. It's almost too much in one little place.'

As a student at the Royal Academy of Music Greenleaves went to concerts by the great orchestras from Vienna, Berlin, Leipzig and Dresden and was struck by the freedom of expression that he perceived in their performances. 'You can't play with your whole soul if your body isn't part of that. If you play with your whole being it's completely different. So that's just one utterly fundamental thing. And the music that was most important to me when I was in my formative years, Bruckner, Strauss, Wagner, Brahms, Schumann, I just always felt that the finest German orchestras were playing it with a different sort of fire in their belly.'

In his third year of studies, he played with the European Youth Orchestra and met the teacher with whom he would study after completing his BMus and a year of postgraduate work. His breakthrough moment at the Academy did not come with a masterclass or a lesson. He adored playing in the orchestras, and loved the atmosphere of the building, but found his formative moments in the library. 'I spent hours and hours and hours and hours with scores and recordings, just sinking into Strauss operas and Bruckner symphonies and Wagner operas, just listening, listening, listening.' He has a horror of delivering mediocre work and, like Rachel Helleur-Simcock and Jo Cole, recognises how vital it is to be mindful of his well-being. 'If I am careful that the condition I am in mentally, emotionally and physically

Opposite and overleaf:
Academy Symphonic Wind
rehearsing in the Duke's Hall

is not too far from the optimum then the work I do really should be considerably better than mediocre.'

The timpanist's job, Greenleaves says, is more complex than holding an orchestra together rhythmically when performances go awry. 'Much more subtle than that is the effect that I can have on the music in exactly how I place my notes', he says. 'If this is a chord, I can join the chord here, here, here or here. None of those places would sound too early or too late but it makes a huge difference. If I'm right at the front of a chord it's a completely different effect. The colour that I can add to the orchestra if I come in just fractionally later, no one will think I was late but how

I place things and the colours I use will influence that sound as a whole.'

The degree to which principal players influence an orchestral performance is a fascinating topic. To what extent are they soloists and to what extent are they part of a body of players? In the Academy Chamber Orchestra's performance of the Haydn overture, flautist Eleanor Blamires, later a participant in Denis Bouriakov's flute masterclass, was employed to lend a rosy tint to the bony, silvery sound of the violins. In the Beethoven symphony, bassoonist Shing To Mak was allowed to change the direction of the conversation and set the tone of the following passage.

'It's chamber music on a very big scale', says Emily Beynon, Principal Flautist with the Royal Concertgebouw Orchestra, Amsterdam. 'One of the things I love about orchestral playing is you are a small cog in a big machine. The repertoire is absolutely overwhelming in its magnitude and its depth, so it feels like a privilege to play in any symphony orchestra and certainly in such a wonderful orchestra in such a great hall. There are moments when one is a soloist but more often than not you're part of a violin group in that line, or you're part of a woodwind chorale there, so the "ears on stalks" aspect is actually one of the things that excites me most about orchestral playing, mixing your sound with other instruments. I love the unity, being part of that whole machine.'

Beynon and Principal Oboist Jonathan Kelly of the Berlin Philharmonic are among the Academy woodwind alumni to have taken positions in mainland Europe. Bouriakov went from playing Principal Flute in the Orchestra of the Metropolitan Opera, New York, to the Los Angeles Philharmonic. Lorna McGhee is Principal Flute with the Pittsburgh Symphony Orchestra.

Bassoonists Rachel Gough and Jonathan Davies, clarinettists Oliver Janes and Timothy Orpen, oboist Tom Blomfield, and flautists Adam Walker, Charlotte Ashton, Amy Yule and Daniel Pailthorpe have remained in the UK, playing as principals with the London Symphony Orchestra, London Philharmonic Orchestra, City of Birmingham Symphony Orchestra, the Orchestra of the Royal Opera House, Aurora Orchestra, the Philharmonia, the BBC Scottish Symphony Orchestra, and the BBC Symphony Orchestra. In terms of the clarinet alone, seven alumni currently hold principal positions in the UK. Douglas Boyd, former Principal Oboe with the Chamber Orchestra of Europe, took another direction altogether, switching mid-career to conducting, and is now Artistic Director of Garsington Opera.

Boyd recalls listening to a performance of a Brahms Sextet on his first day at the Academy and realising that, although he had been a 'star' in the Glasgow Youth Orchestra, this was another world. It was a 'light-bulb moment' in which he realised what he needed to do to reach that level. Excellent tuition from the 'quietly inspiring and quietly tough' Janet Craxton, masterclasses with Maurice Bourgue and, like Greenleaves, 'devouring concerts' propelled his technical development and musical tastes. In the early days of the Chamber Orchestra of Europe, he says, 'we shared the belief that playing with the orchestra was not a job but a privilege, that one played every performance as if it was one's last, and that this commitment and passion were equalled by the search for musical excellence.'

Orpen, too, was slightly stunned as a fresher by the quality of the playing of his fellow students. 'At the time I thought I must have been pretty good to get into the Academy, but after hearing the performance of an outstanding Russian clarinettist in the class I realised how much work I needed to do in order to compete with students from around the world. Eavesdropping outside his practice room was also a valuable lesson!' Walker's first impression, aged seventeen, was of 'a sense of occasion. There were always people around. It felt like a hub of activity, students, staff and the public, and felt like a venue as well as a conservatoire', he says. 'Straight away I fed off the energy around me, socially and musically. Collaboration is so important for musicians.'

Both players work as soloists, chamber musicians and orchestral musicians. Learning how to switch modes, as

Matthew Gee observed, is critical. Walker remembers stepping in for a friend in an orchestral repertoire session on Prokofiev's *Romeo and Juliet* with Colin Metters, then Head of Conducting. After he played the brooding, curving flute melody, Metters told him to 'make it a solo, to draw people in' rather than simply play the notes on the page. 'This one sentence taught me a lot about projection – how it wasn't purely a question of dynamic but of colour, purpose and intent, something which I try to pass on to my students today', he says. His own teacher, Michael Cox, told him there is no set rule for knowing when to back off. 'Use your radar' was his advice, much like Beynon's orchestral maxim of having to have your 'ears on stalks'.

Ashton, now Principal Flute with the BBC Scottish Symphony Orchestra, was 'quite shocked' when the orchestral excerpts she had learned were put in context. 'In a young flute player's mind, they become the "defining feature" of the works from which they are taken. *Daphnis et Chloé* becomes "the one with the huge flute solo", *Peter and the Wolf* becomes "the one with lots of little technical flute solos", *Till Eulenspiegel* becomes "the one with the pesky dovetailing flute duet"', she says. For the first few months of my job, I spent my time poring over the schedule looking for all the pieces I recognised. I soon realised that all instrumentalists' perspectives are different. *Peter and the Wolf* is "the one where everyone has a difficult part" and *Till Eulenspiegel* is "the one with the huge horn solos"!'

Ashton's experience playing in a wind quintet throughout her time at the Academy proved crucial. 'It was where I learned the indispensable skill of blending my sound with the other instruments of the wind section in terms of

Strings Gallery in the Academy's museum

Bass clarinet student
in rehearsal

vibrato and colour. It was building my stamina, teaching me to lead a chamber group and ultimately increasing my confidence to start leading a wind section, and allowing a platform for creativity, experimenting with different phrasings, balances and dynamics. All of this stood me in good stead for the orchestral world. There isn't a working day when I don't put into practice something that I learnt from my quintet.'

As to the difference between playing on a concert stage or in the pit of a theatre, Orpen says that while the concentration and stamina required in playing long operas week after week in the Royal Opera House is intense and demanding, 'the extreme sensitivity of rubato and dynamics through working with great singers over the years' is a quality he loves in that orchestra. The contrast with his work with Aurora, which includes playing symphonies from memory, sometimes with props, costumes and lighting effects, is something he values: 'The early years of Aurora were supported by the Academy, which was a great help as we were basically a bunch of students trying to start a new orchestra in a city with too many orchestras already. If you'd have told people back then that we'd soon be playing at the BBC Proms they would have laughed!'

In the glass-fronted luthiers' workshop on the first floor of the Academy's museum in York Gate the pigments are arranged in little pots on the shelf: Siena, Cadmium, Orange and Magister Madder; Indian Red, Indian Yellow and Alizarin Crimson; Lamp Black, Mars Black and Ivory

Black. There are only a handful of places in Europe that offer training in this craft, which is peaceful and painstaking and practical.

Today two instruments are being restored by Ijmkje van der Werf and Anja Kuch: a Viennese violin that was made around 1840 and has sustained scuffs on its edgework, and one from Cremona that was made in the early 1790s, its varnish in need of attention with tiny brushstrokes. Just as a violin will leave its marks on a player, from the telltale bruise under their jaw to the flattened tips of the fingers of their left hand, players leave their marks on violins. The varnish on the back of the Cremonese instrument has worn away where it touches its player's shoulder.

Good work cannot be rushed. Both instruments will remain in the workshop for two or three days. From violins to violas, cellos, lutes, viols and guitars from the eighteenth to the early twentieth century, the instruments that pass through the workshop are played day in and day out, 'not hung on the wall like a painting', as Kuch says.

In addition to maintaining the Academy's prestigious collection of 240 instruments and 180 historical bows, the Curator of Instruments Barbara Meyer and Instrument Loans Co-Ordinator Sheldon Gabriel act as matchmakers. As Jo Cole hinted earlier, there can be tears when it is time for a student to hand back a cherished instrument – an anecdote that any pianist who has encountered a substandard piano while touring a concert programme will greet with a raised eyebrow. Alumnus Steven Isserlis still plays the Academy's Marquis de Corberon Stradivarius cello, after which his visiting professorship is named.

Museum Curator Gabrielle Gale studied saxophone and oboe at the Academy, and soon after became a member of the quartet the Fairer Sax, before changing career. She now oversees the permanent and temporary exhibitions in the galleries. While some of the most precious and rare stringed instruments – a violin, viola and cello by Antonio Stradivari – are stored behind glass at 50 to 60 per cent humidity and a temperature of 18 to 21 degrees, the museum is both open to the public and an active performance, rehearsal and outreach space.

A portrait of the virtuoso violinist Niccolò Paganini underlines what Gale describes as the 'symbiotic relationship between player, maker and composer' that informs the technological and aesthetic changes in the history of musical instruments. Within each display case is a longer history: the tree from which Stradivari made the Archinto viola in 1696 was probably planted in the fourteenth century.

There are sociological developments too: a baroque guitar chastely shaped to be fit for a respectable female amateur, its curves less suggestive of a human body, and a painting of a group of sisters in an Austenesque interior with a square fortepiano. Research fellows and Masters students play the keyboard instruments located on the second floor, which trace the development of plucked and struck technology across three centuries.

The collection includes a 1787 Broadwood with a Venetian swell mechanism, a six-pedal 1815 Heichele piano with a buzzing bassoon stop and the Turkish cymbal and bell effects that were then in vogue in Vienna, and an 1880 Érard grand with a rosewood case and a dreamily transparent tone. Some of these instruments were intended for domestic, rather than public, use.

With the advent of recording technology, the ubiquity of the pianoforte in the living room was eroded, and with it, the hegemony of the Western art music tradition. On the ground floor, among the scores and letters and batons of famous visitors, a cartoon from the 19 July 1922 edition of *Punch* magazine catches the eye: the drawing depicts the Academy in its centenary year, with the title 'Promise and Fulfillment'.

It is the closing weekend of the EFG London Jazz Festival, an annual celebration of more than a hundred years of jazz, from trad to experimental, bebop to ambient, in venues across the city. Onstage in the Clore Ballroom of the Royal Festival Hall saxophonist Tim Garland and the Academy Big Band have just begun their set. The crowd that spills out to the Long Bar is a mixture of young families with toddlers, hip singletons and older jazz aficionados.

The music curls and blossoms like hothouse flowers in vivid shades of violet, indigo, mustard and scarlet, a closely harmonised secular Sanctus. What would the readers of that 1922 jazz age edition of *Punch* make of this? At the back of the dance floor trumpeter Nick Smart, Head of Jazz at the Academy, is watching his students, nodding from time to time.

A technical glitch from the festival sound desk requires a restart. 'For those of you who are interested we are going from bar 257', announces Garland smoothly. Student Harry Baker's piano solo unfolds as something between an ecstatic love song and a lament. Considering the richness and intensity of the harmonies of brass, keyboards, guitar and wind, the ensemble is extraordinarily light and tight, pricked through with the pop and shimmer from Luca Caruso's drum kit.

The music curls
and blossoms like
hothouse flowers
in vivid shades
of violet, indigo,
mustard and scarlet,
a closely harmonised
secular Sanctus.

Garland has already played one gig in the festival at the 606 Club with the pianist and Academy alumnus and professor Gwilym Simcock. Saxophonist and alumna Trish Clowes and her quartet, My Iris, have played there too this week. Alumnus Kit Downes, pianist, harmonium and organ player, will be performing at Kansas Smitty's in Hackney the next day, at about the same time as Smart's Academy All Stars – a band of former students including rising trumpeters Steve Fishwick and Freddie Gavita and the legendary seventy-eight-year-old Henry Lowther, who studied violin at the Academy and played at Woodstock with Keef Hartley – play Gil Evans's recently rediscovered arrangement of the score to *Porgy and Bess* at St John's Smith Square under Smart's direction.

Smart, who is playing with the Whirlwind Orchestra straight after Garland's set, is the third person to run the Academy Jazz Department since its foundation in 1989 by the bass player and composer Graham Collier. It is a small and ambitious department and students are expected to be able to work in ensemble classes with artists like Nikki Iles from their first term onwards.

The discipline and heritage are distinct from other departments in the Academy. 'Mark David wouldn't want one of my trumpet players in the orchestra having a go

at Mahler for the first time with Sir Simon Rattle', says Smart.

'It's like the difference between an African drummer and a timpanist. It's the tradition that they've come from. The sound they make is different because it belongs to a different lineage. The requirements of what you're expected to bring to the music are different – especially whenever there is improvisation involved. It's expected that you bring more in the way of personality and inventiveness and something that might change the course of the music as an improviser, whereas if you're playing a trumpet part in Mahler you're supposed to do that brilliantly and do that in a very informed and stylistically nuanced way, but you're not meant to change the direction of the symphony.'

Proactive membership of the International Association of Schools of Jazz and collaborations with the Frost School of Music in Miami have ensured Smart's department has an international profile. So, too, has the success of alumni including Jacob Collier, Ashley Henry, Sarah Tandy, Clowes, Fishwick, Gavita, Simcock and Downes, and projects like the

ECM label celebrations in 2020, with guest artists such as Evan Parker and Norma Winstone.

Smart has seen 'an explosion of degree-level jazz education' in specialist secondary schools over the last two decades, and his first-year students are already operating at a very high level in terms of technique and knowledge when they arrive. Nonetheless, he says, 'genuine individual flair and personality, self-expression in the music, that is still rare'.

Listening forms a central part of the training on the jazz course, what Smart calls 'the deep listening of learning a solo off by heart, from memory, without writing it down, and playing along with the recording to the point that you can't put a piece of paper between you and the original'. Another key component is composition. 'The amount of composition in the Jazz Department is equal to if not more than the amount of composition in the Composition Department. They are all composing all the time, and that does have an impact on their sense of community. It fast-tracks that musical connection where you're playing each other's

Jazz students rehearse with Chris Potter (above) and Dave Holland (left)

Opposite: Jazz students in rehearsal in the Susie Sainsbury Theatre

material. You're bonding in a different way. It's an almost accidentally beautiful thing about the department.'

The African-American roots of jazz 'have to be front and centre of your education' Smart says, but a glance at the EFG Festival brochure gives a sense of the variety of musical styles, nuances, techniques and traditions the students have to absorb. 'This guy phoned up who was furious about a very free and avant-garde concert we did. I said, "Come back and hear them play Benny Goodman! You have to understand we're preparing the students for all of this, not just the bit you love." That is a result of the fact that jazz, as a word, means so many things.' Dave Holland, Miles Davis's last bass player, is among the luminaries to teach in Smart's department.

Kit Downes attended the Junior Academy jazz course for a few years prior to joining the undergraduate course from the Purcell School and describes Smart as 'one of the most important and inspiring teachers I've ever had'. Downes still plays regularly with the drummers James Maddren and Joshua Blackmore and the guitarist Chris Montague, whom he met on his first day as a student. 'It was brilliant to be around so many musicians my own age that were already so committed to the music. There was immediately a feeling of community within the jazz course, and also an atmosphere of rigour and practice.'

Courses, classes and lessons with Jason Rebello, the late John Taylor, Tom Cawley, Nikki Iles, Gwilym Simcock and a masterclass with the US trio, Fly, had a lasting impact on Downes, who was then finding it challenging to play with freedom at the same time as learning the tools with which to express himself. 'I was lucky enough to be picked to play a tune with Larry Grenadier and Jeff Ballard as a trio. I was so nervous that I got lost on a blues, within about six bars – pretty lame. At the time it was completely devastating as they were my heroes and I felt like I blew it, but on talking to Jeff Ballard afterwards he told me that it was really because

I stopped listening that that happened. "Listening is always your way back into the music", he said.'

Barak Schmool's World Rhythms class 'opened the door for so many different approaches – rhythmically, harmonically, compositionally – and did so through so many different types of music. He really helped me see the various common strands that link them together', says Downes. The transition from student to professional was blurry, as it is for many musicians. 'I guess it's really about experience – performing, preparing, creating, teaching – all things that I felt prepared and excited for in my last year of college.'

Simcock, too, arrived from a specialist school, Chetham's in Manchester, and is now a professor at the Academy. 'Having studied mainly classical music for nine years, enrolling on the specialist jazz course at the Academy was a very exciting feeling. Being around some wonderful musicians, all dedicated to the same style of music as myself, was definitely a special feeling. The course is well known as being probably the best in the country, and the small size of the course – basically a "band" of musicians in each year – makes it a very intimate and focused group of students.' One of the great benefits of the course, he says, is that 'students get to work with their heroes and, if they are up to the task, then they will eventually be hired and get to work with them in the "real world", as what we do really doesn't have any age limitations.'

He has toured all over the world with the electric bassist Laurence Cottle, whom he met in his second year when Cottle came in to work with the Academy Big Band. 'I'd obsessed over a recording of him playing with his quintet from when I first heard it back at school a few years earlier, so to have him come in and play some of the same music with us was a massive thrill.' Classes with Garland also led to their working together, and the experience of teaching

'Students get to work
with their heroes and,
if they are up to the task,
then they will eventually
be hired and get to
work with them in the
"real world"'

Downes's year group led Simcock to invite Maddren to play with him. 'I really think our little musical world is very much like a family', he says, 'and the Academy has definitely been a huge part of mine since I started here in 1999.' Now Downes is on the staff in the department too. 'I enjoy teaching quite a few classical students who are interested in improvising and harmony – and I know a few jazz students taking classical lessons', he says. 'I think this cross-talk is really healthy for both scenes.'

Downes sees the jazz and classical courses as 'part of the same big picture'. Where there is a strong technical and aesthetic connection to the Jazz Department, as Smart acknowledges, is in much of the work that is done in Historical Performance. Just as Smart's students would be expected to be able to improvise on a standard from the American Songbook, the lutenist Elizabeth Kenny's students, and those of harpsichord continuo professor Pawel Siwczak, must learn to improvise on the passacaglias and chaconnes that are the backbone of baroque music. As the violinist and head of the Historical Performance Department Margaret Faultless puts it, 'We don't play what's on the page, and neither do the jazzers.'

'If you're playing Mahler's Second Symphony, you have to play what's on the page', continues Faultless. 'Obviously, you can't just go in there and play what's on the page and

that will be enough. But the parameters of what you do with the material are fixed in a different way, and I always say to people, with most repertoire, heading really quite late, well into the nineteenth century, rule number one is don't play what's on the page. Then the question is, how do you know which bits of what's not on the page you play?'

Watching Kenny improvise with her third-year undergraduate student Sergio Bucheli on a ground bass by Purcell and a dance from Robert de Visée's Suite in D Minor, stretching and teasing the rhythms, is not so very different from watching Nikki Iles coach a seven-piece band of Smart's first-year students through Keith Jarrett's 'The Journey Home' or Downes's recollection of playing with John Taylor as a student and realising that Taylor was 'teaching me to teach myself'.

Kenny estimates that improvisation makes up approximately 50 per cent of her work as a lutenist. As a teacher, she spends the first year with a student working on finding a sound and being very conscious of that sound, building improvisational skills once the student's technique is secure. Like Smart, Walker and Beynon, she emphasises the importance of listening.

'To be able to listen while you're playing is massively important on any instrument, but it's quite particular to playing continuo on the lute because you have to get the playing processes unconscious enough that you can just be thinking about the orchestra or the singer or the violinist in front of you. That's very similar to piano accompaniment but with the added factor that you also have to make decisions about how many notes you're going to play or what sort of chord you're going to play if you're improvising. You need to have quite a lot of spare brain space for that so you can't be worried about where the fourth fret is.'

Minute alterations of gesture and articulation can have an extraordinary impact, musically and visually. There

Overleaf: Ryan Wigglesworth conducting the Academy Symphony Orchestra's
performance of Sir Michael Tippett's *The Rose Lake* in the Duke's Hall in 2018

'We have a relationship with history as musicians unless we're doing free-form improvisation in the moment, and even that is informed by what we've studied before.'

is as much theatre in the silence at the end of Kenny's and Bucheli's arm movements as there is in the different sounds produced by plucking or strumming with fingers or thumb. Just as a student in the Jazz Department might be a singer, a brass player, a flautist, a clarinettist, a keyboard player, a guitarist or a percussionist, Faultless's students play 'anything from horn, sackbutt, recorder, bassoon, flute or any of the historical stringed instruments, clavichord, fortepiano, harpsichord and chamber organ'.

Alongside first-study instrumental lessons, the course offers dance classes, lessons in rhetoric, classes on current debates in musicology and on performance practice. 'There's very little duplication of activities, and everybody's personalities can really come to the fore', says Faultless. An interest in historical performance did not seem unusual to her when she was growing up. 'My mother played in a group with David Munrow. It wasn't weird. I grew up with the harpsichord alongside the grand piano, and the recorders. It wasn't peculiar. My father sang Dowland or Vaughan Williams. He didn't sing everything in the same way, and that seemed natural to me.'

'I studied recorder and piano with my mother, and violin with a number of teachers, but I don't ever remember a fight about it. I just remember being interested in thinking about how to play, and I suppose that I found people who were thinking as I was, who happened to have put gut strings on their instruments.' After specialising in contemporary music, Faultless became a central figure in the early music revival of the 1980s, working with Roger Norrington, Christopher Hogwood, Andrew Parrott and Ton Koopman, and leading the Orchestra of the Age of Enlightenment.

Historical practice has long ceased to be a niche interest. There are sixty students studying period instruments as a second study, as Adam Walker did with the baroque flautist, Lisa Beznosiuk. Alumna Anneke Scott, who specialises in

historical horns, is among the recent success stories from the Academy. Faultless has a pragmatic attitude to her field. 'History informs a lot of what we do as performers – whether it's what your teacher told you and what their teacher told them, whether it's listening to recordings that could have been made over a great length of time, whether it's using editions that were compiled yesterday or 200 years ago, whether it's playing on instruments that were built to modern specifications or on instruments that are older', she says.

'We have a relationship with history as musicians unless we're doing free-form improvisation in the moment, and even that is informed by what we've studied before. So I find it much more interesting to think about how much history is informing what you do, not whether history is informing what you do. In an institution like the Academy, people are encouraged to think on many levels about how they play and why they play. I encourage my students, all of whom have opted to use some aspects of historical technology – gut strings, no chin rest, period bows – to think especially hard about that. In a funny way, that's the only difference between them and anybody else.'

Where the modern and period instrument students come together is in the Bach Cantatas series, now in its twelfth year. The overall scheme came about through the vision and generosity of the late Sir Ralph Kohn. This, and his friendship with Freeman-Attwood, led to all the cantatas being performed over ten years. Now the harpsichordist and organist John Butt, author of the most accessible book on historical performance practice of recent years, *Playing with History* (2002), and Founder and Director of the Dunedin Consort, is helping Freeman-Attwood forge a new series, 'Bach the European', which will also celebrate the tercentenary of Bach's first cycle of cantatas in 1723. Visiting conductors include Masaaki Suzuki and Philippe Herreweghe, and the repertoire has expanded to reflect music by Bach's predecessors and contemporaries.

Some concerts are blended, with first- and second-study players sharing desks in the orchestra. 'Within the string and wind players there are some who are already of international standard and their expertise and style very usefully "infect" those who are less experienced', observes Butt. 'So the atmosphere and outlook have been great on the instrumental side and there's a real sense of professionalism and style, even from those who are still stronger on the "modern" instruments.'

It is not just instrumentalists who benefit from this intensive introduction to baroque music. Soprano Jennifer France, an emerging star in operatic repertoire from Handel to Strauss and Brett Dean to Gerald Barry, found a musical home in the Bach Cantatas series as a postgraduate student. 'These Sunday morning concerts were truly some of my favourite times at the Academy', she says. 'Getting to sing so much Bach on a regular basis not only helped me secure my vocal technique, but also working with the Academy Baroque Orchestra under Iain Ledingham's direction was inspiring, and I still perform regularly with many of my friends from the orchestra, in other orchestras such as the Academy of Ancient Music.' Tenor Thomas Hobbs is another distinguished

alumnus of the series, singing the Evangelist all over the world, and Academy graduates populate many of the finest European baroque orchestras as leaders and obbligato soloists.

Tenor Ed Lyon, whose most recent recording, with Elizabeth Kenny, is *17th Century Playlist*, points out that he might sing music by Francesco Cavalli, Bach, Mozart, Beethoven, Wagner, Strauss, Britten and Thomas Adès in a single season. 'In the 1980s and '90s, early music was considered a specialists' game', he says. 'Now I think my generation of singers are expected to have a varied repertoire. There are few I can think of outside of the "lyric Italianate" type who haven't sung some Handel, Bach or Monteverdi.' Listening to Ledingham rehearse the vocal consort for the December performance of *Das neugeborne Kindelein*, BWV 69a, part of the 'Bach the European' series, the flexibility of the students' voices is impressive.

'What is striking is the range of backgrounds', says Butt. 'Some already have choral or early music experience but hope to develop into more mainstream soloists, and some have relatively little experience of consort singing but are very keen on learning more of baroque style. The big challenge for me is to rehearse the singers enough so that they are secure and stylish, but not so much that they actually lose their voices. A real triumph for all was de Lalande's *De Profundis*. Some of the singers and players had some experience of French baroque style, but by no means all. Given that much of it was technically relatively straightforward, we could work on the style, rhythm and inflection of this music and I think the results were excellent.'

The more time you spend in the Academy building, the stronger the impression that everything is connected, whether the instrument is period or modern, stringed, brass, woodwind, keyboard, percussion, whether the repertoire

Stephen Sondheim in conversation with Jonathan Freeman-Attwood following the presentation of his Honorary Doctorate

is a standard from the American Songbook, a Bach Suite, a Chopin Prelude, a baroque toccata or fanfare, a string quartet, samba or symphony. When students are waiting for a lesson or a rehearsal, they practise where they can, playing in the band room or – a favourite with the brass players, despite the limited space – the locker room. The portability of an instrument has surprisingly little impact on where you might find someone playing it. For every ad hoc guitarist in a corridor, there is an ad hoc double bassist.

Cole's survival guide encourages British students to reach out to international freshers. The student body of 800 includes musicians from around sixty different countries across Western and Eastern Europe, North, Central and South America, Australia and the Far East. It must be especially hard as an incomer, however, when your instrument is not part of a standard orchestral set-up. Yet the success of accordionists Martynas Levickis and Ksenija Sidorova, who hold recording contracts with Decca and Deutsche Grammophon respectively, suggests there may be benefits to studying as part of a small department. Guitarist Miloš Karadaglić was barely seventeen when he arrived as a student in 2000. The move from Montenegro to London was

'like landing on Mars', he says. 'This was scary but it was all I ever wanted. On the one hand, I was heartbroken to have left my family. On the other, I was beyond excited – and even more terrified – for everything that was to come.'

After ten years of guitar tuition at Bejing's Central Conservatoire, Xuefei Yang was struck by the individuality that was encouraged at the Royal Academy of Music. 'I felt that the teachers and students were international, so their thinking and backgrounds were all different, which was fascinating for me', she says. 'Lots of the students were quite independent in terms of knowing what they wanted, and in their thinking. At the Academy we had more choices in choosing repertoire, and more freedom in how we wanted to play, and what we wanted to do.'

Both Yang and Karadaglić studied with Michael Lewin, who had taught Kenny in Junior Academy. 'He never tried to change my instincts, but instead always tried to help me find the best sounds I had hidden inside', says Karadaglić. 'This gave me confidence and the tools to carve my own musical path.' The smallness of the department turned out to be an advantage, according to Yang, who relished the opportunity to focus on chamber music.

Opposite: The Academy's Musical Theatre Company with Imelda Staunton on Graduation Day

'It was a dream', says Karadaglić. 'We were like family, always collaborating, exchanging ideas and musical opinions. My favourite part was the play-throughs we organised ahead of any major concert. It was just a few of us and we got on really well. We also formed ensembles and various chamber combinations. It was incredibly inspiring, immersive, joyous and often mischievous. I miss those days very much.'

The transition from student to professional is 'the toughest part of any musician's life' warns Karadaglić. 'The bare reality of what being a musician means hits you hard, and in London it hits you very, very hard. The one thing that helped me immensely was the Junior Fellowship. It allowed me to stay close to the Academy for two years after finishing my Masters course. This was a soft, warm cushion against the cold, cruel world. I will forever be grateful for

that.' Twenty years into her career as a soloist, Yang says the most valuable lesson she has learned is self-determination: 'I realise more and more that I am the most important manager of my own career.'

Threading through every department in the Academy are the research projects undertaken by professors, postgraduates and PhD students. These range from critical analyses of the collaborative process to a study of Messiaen's *Cahiers des chants d'oiseaux*, the preparation of a critical edition of Fauré's songs, a microanalysis of Mozart's developing style, a survey of jazz pedagogy in Europe, the commission of new instruments and new music, and the production of scores, books and recordings. The diversity of potential career paths extends beyond the titles of soloist, chamber musician, orchestral musician or singer. Canadian pianist Allyson Devenish came as a postgraduate to study lieder

accompaniment and now balances recital work with composing, arranging, producing, researching and playwriting and her role as Music Director of NitroVoX. Violinist Andrew Manze is now a conductor. Singing students Gareth Malone, Aled Jones and Katherine Jenkins have found roles in broadcasting and popular culture.

The singer-songwriter Annie Lennox, who arrived at the Academy as a flautist, achieved fame in the 1980s with the Eurythmics before striking out as a solo artist. In 2019 the most famous alumnus of Junior Academy, Sir Elton John, launched his autobiography, *Me*, in the Duke's Hall, in front of the Sir Elton John and Ray Cooper organ, a handsome instrument built by Orgelbau Kuhn in clean, modern counterpoint to the Edwardian architecture. Downstairs in the student bar there is a more humble tribute: Sir Elton Gin is the first item on the cocktail list.

In terms of renewing the conservatoire tradition internationally, the alumni who have become educators, administrators, managers and artistic directors play vital roles: Clive Gillinson, former Managing Director of the London Symphony Orchestra and current Artistic Director of Carnegie Hall, New York; Phillippa Cole, Director of Artistic Planning at the San Francisco Symphony; Amelia Freedman, Founder and Artistic Director of The Nash Ensemble; Linda Merrick, Principal of the Royal Northern College of Music; George Caird, former Principal of the Royal Birmingham Conservatoire and Royal Welsh College of Music and Drama, and former Director of Classical Music at Codarts, Rotterdam; Nick Mathias, Global Artistic Management Consultant with IMG Artists; and Gaetan Le Divelec, Director at Askonas Holt arts management.

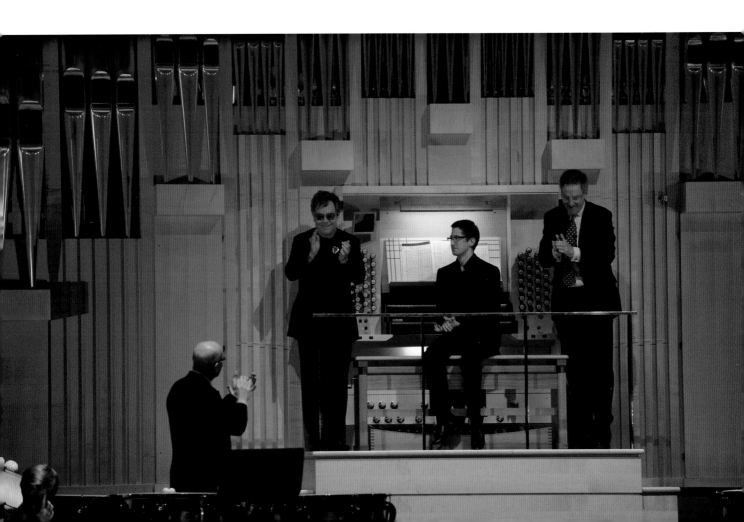

Mathias studied violin at the Academy. 'It was where my musical journey really started, where I came under the spell', he says. A career as an orchestral violinist seemed to be the obvious choice. He was a member of the Bournemouth Symphony Orchestra for six years before moving into management with the Royal Liverpool Philharmonic and the Ulster Orchestras, returning to Bournemouth as Concerts Director, planning concert programmes and working closely with the conductors and soloists he engaged. 'I always felt I had a special affinity with conductors, and just as I was giving some thought to what my next move might be, I was approached about moving into artist management in London with one of the key agencies, specialising in the management of conductors.' Twenty-five years on, he works with conductors including Antonio Pappano, Vasily Petrenko and Vladimir Jurowski.

As a young clarinettist, Merrick says that 'the Academy gave me a love of chamber music and contemporary music' and encouraged her to develop her own projects with peers. She now balances a performing career with her work at the Royal Northern College of Music: 'I think the focus, commitment and dedication required to achieve excellence as a performer or composer, and the quality and breadth of training you receive at a top conservatoire, are hugely beneficial in a leadership role. This background helps you to think strategically, to identify creative solutions to problems, to work independently in a focused way, to lead and motivate colleagues, to be highly organised and structured, and to be ambitious for your institution and everyone associated with it. It also gives you the personal resilience you need in such a complex and challenging role.'

Caird's early experiences as an oboe student at the Academy and, later, as Head of Woodwind and Orchestral Studies, give a sense of how tightly interwoven tradition and innovation can be. His teacher, Janet Craxton, gave the first performances of works by Elisabeth Lutyens, Priaulx Rainier, Jean Françaix and Witold Lutoslawski. Harmony lessons with John Gardner covered works from Josquin des Prez to Sorabji; Nadia Boulanger gave classes as a visiting professor.

Caird's fellow students included Sir Simon Rattle, Dame Felicity Lott, Graham Johnson, Monica Huggett and Raphael Wallfisch. 'I remember many exciting performances in the Duke's Hall including *Ein Heldenleben* and Shostakovich's Tenth Symphony, but perhaps the most inspirational was the 150th Anniversary concert at the Royal Festival Hall with Clifford Curzon playing Mozart's Piano Concerto K 595 exquisitely. Remembering Curzon turning to play with the woodwind players on the stage of the RFH in that concert was a true inspiration.'

He watched the growth of the Early Music revival and the beginning of an institutional engagement with new work that would lead to the Academy's composer festivals in the 1980s. In hindsight, he says, his training 'was more of an apprenticeship than a course'. He was thrilled to contribute to the woodwind syllabus when the first BMus course was introduced, followed by the MMus and PhD courses.

'The thinking behind all this is profound', says Caird. 'Musicians – and all artists – pursue work which is of matching value to traditional academics. Furthermore, the overlap between artistic and academic achievement is a seamless continuum where each individual can find their own position. The design of conservatoire degrees across the world has been an extraordinary adventure and it would be fair to say that conservatoires have very much led the way in developing degrees that can mirror the gifts of the individual.'

Every head of department emphasises versatility. The portfolio career is not new. Think of Handel: composer, keyboard virtuoso, impresario, teacher. Music for television, cinema, games and social-media advertising has become a lucrative 'side hustle' but cannot provide the financial

Opposite: from left to right, Ray Cooper, Sir Elton John, Peter Holder and Jonathan Freeman-Attwood at the unveiling of the Duke's Hall organ

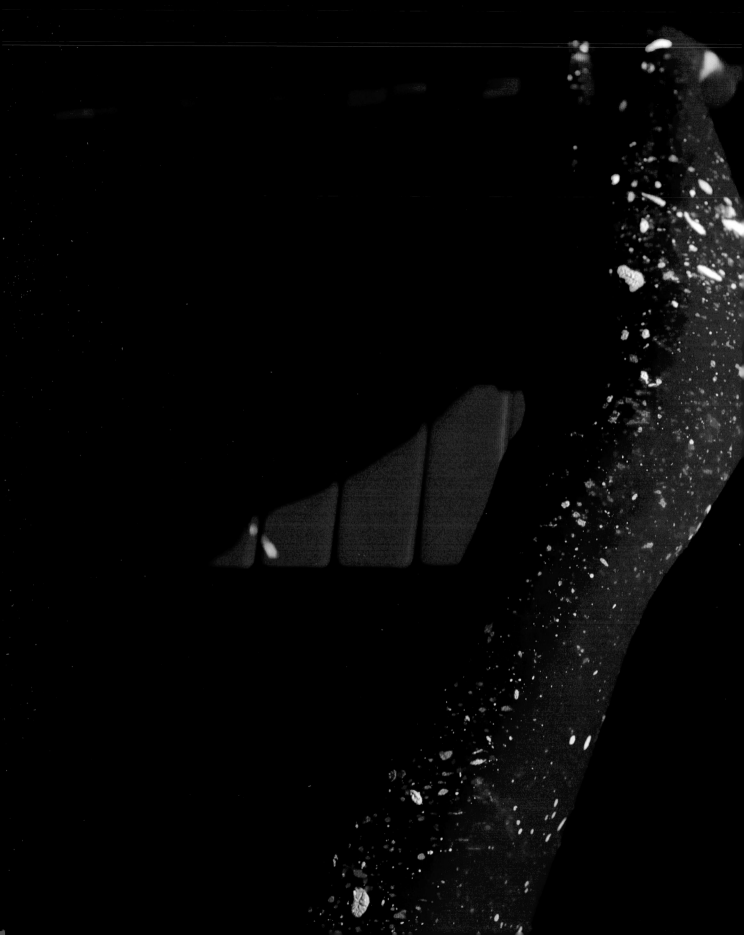

security once offered by recording contracts, especially those issued in the first decade of compact disc production, when every label commissioned symphony cycles and complete works on period and modern instruments.

Not a year goes past without a press release claiming that this or that studio recording will be the last of its type. Singers, instrumental soloists, ensembles and orchestras, many of which have their own labels, are now more likely to have to find their own funding to make recordings than they are to be paid to make those recordings.

Outreach, learning and participation projects have become central to the work of venues, opera companies, orchestras and smaller ensembles in recent years: a way of connecting with members of the community who would not otherwise have access to classical music, and a further discipline for the modern musician to learn.

Open Academy, the Academy's long-established community arm run by Julian West, serves three functions: taking music out of the building to primary and secondary schools, to the Royal London and Chelsea and Westminster Hospitals, to residential care homes and the City Lit Percussion Orchestra; bringing the community into the building with projects such as Academy Tots and Weekend Vocal Workouts; and training students to facilitate these projects.

The by-product of this experience is invaluable, as West says: 'Students can, through that training, rediscover play in the sense of experimenting, playing and having fun. It is easy to lose that through a conservatoire training. It taps back into that initial desire to be a musician and what music means to them.' West teaches two elective undergraduate courses and one elective postgraduate course and considers it his role to encourage musicians to think beyond performing or teaching. Trumpeter Hannah Opstad, cellist Hermione Jones, flautist Alyson Frazier and composer James Moriarty are among the Academy alumni whose imagination was caught by their Open Academy experiences and who now work in socially engaged or 'applied music'.

West's own area of interest is in music as a means of supporting health and well-being, particularly in the field of dementia. 'There's a huge amount of research into how music can access memory. The way in which we perceive and process music doesn't happen in just one part of the brain. It draws on lots of different areas', he says.

'The work that I'm involved in is very much focused on improvisation and making new music alongside people who have dementia, kind of thinking about how if someone is struggling with memory then let's not worry about memory, let's work in the present. This is about music that we are making, here and now. As musicians we can respond to gesture and we can make something together. It's that process of attempting to make something together that forges a connection.'

In the 1980s the talent of many of the students at the Academy had been fostered by free instrumental tuition from local education authorities. Brass players often hailed from mining villages where the brass-band tradition was maintained with vigour and pride. With the progressive reduction of funding for arts education, an emphasis on STEM subjects in the school curriculum and the 'weaponisation' of the word 'elite', current students at the Academy, many of them from specialist music schools, can feel nervous going into local schools for the first time.

'Their assumption is that the young people won't like the music they play, that they won't think it's relevant, that they're only interested in electronic music', says West. 'More often than not they are surprised at the warmth of the reception they get. Just this week we were working in a local secondary school and the young people at the school absolutely loved it and really appreciated the musicianship. The shock is usually a very pleasant one.'

How do you maintain an instrument that is invisible?

Much of the exposure to composition and performance at primary school level depends on the experience of the teachers. West points to one example of a school where the resident music specialist is a trumpeter and every Year 3 cohort becomes a brass band. 'In other schools it won't be as rich an experience', he admits. Are schemes like Open Academy an attempt to fix a broken limb with a sticking plaster? 'No, I don't think so', he says. 'I think it's much more about the students broadening their sense of themselves and who they are in the world, so some of the work is about engaging with young people who wouldn't have access to the kind of musical experiences that are on offer here or in other cultural venues. It's about engaging with young people's innate creativity, with their musicality, with their musicianship, and validating it.'

How do you maintain an instrument that is invisible? A strong stomach is required to view a film of a laryngoscopy and an even stronger one is needed when you are the patient. Oyster-like in appearance, the larynx only makes itself felt when it is in trouble, something that Kate Paterson, Head of Vocal Studies, and Professor Yvonne Howard teach their students to avoid. As Paterson points out, there are several approaches to teaching vocal technique. Some are physically based, with a focus on anatomical terminology; others rely on imagery. Matchmaking students and teachers is a major part of her job. For the rest, she concentrates on instilling professional values.

'In order to work you've got to be a lot of things', she says. 'You have to be a great colleague. You have to be professional. You have to be personable. You have to have your audition arias ready to go at the drop of a hat. And you have to be great on stage. I think the modern singer is a very different beast. You need to jump in and have a go. You need to be able to do physical stuff. You need to be entertaining. You need to be good in music and drama. You have to have an excellent technique in order to survive but on top of that you need to have all these other attributes that are geared to getting people into work – whatever that work is.'

Howard, whose repertoire extends from Beethoven, Britten and bel canto to verismo and contemporary opera, echoes Paterson's emphasis on flexibility. 'We spend a lot of time working on technique, interpretation, languages and performance, but there are so many other aspects to a future career that only experience can teach a person and so I feel it is up to me to make my students aware of how any potential pitfalls may affect them emotionally and vocally. The toolkit a singer needs to carry with them is quite a heavily laden one.'

As with many performers who are also teachers, she has found the experience joyful. 'I feel jolly lucky', she says. 'I learn so much from working with my students. I truly think that the whole teaching experience has helped keep my own singing on track due to the analysing and problem-solving we do together.'

Alumni from this department are highly visible on the concert platform, in oratorio and in opera. Jennifer France, Christina Gansch, Ed Lyon, David Butt Philip, Christopher Maltman, Marcus Farnsworth, Neal Davies, Emma Bell, Iestyn Davies, Brindley Sherratt, Jean Rigby, Sarah Tynan, Allan Clayton, Peter Bronder, Robin Tritschler, Rupert Charlesworth, Alex Otterburn, Mary Bevan, Sam Furness and Hilary Summers have distinguished themselves not by focusing on one musical form or style but by their versatility.

Lucy Crowe's repertoire extends from Handel to Mozart, Donizetti, Verdi, Strauss and Janáček, often in stagings that involve a great deal of physical movement. If a gear change is required between completing her run at the Royal Opera House in Barrie Kosky's production of *Agrippina* and giving a masterclass on music by Donizetti, Britten, Stravinksy, Bellini and Massenet in the Angela Burgess Recital Hall it does not show.

'It is a privilege for me to be invited back to the Academy to give masterclasses. I am learning from them and enjoying them hugely', she says. 'I was brilliantly nurtured when I studied here, and to be given the opportunity to give a little bit back, to play some small part in the education of the next generation of opera singers, is very special.'

'Wow! Goodness me! See you at Covent Garden!' is Crowe's first response to soprano Kathleen Nic Dhiarmada's account of 'Prendi per me sei libero'. The aria is a turning point for Adina, the heroine of Donizetti's *L'elisir d'amore*, and the moment in which she admits her love for Nemorino, the childhood friend who has been hopelessly and secretly in love with her for years.

The opera is a comedy, and one of a precious handful with a workable moral: that a little of what you fancy does you good. Crowe encourages Nic Dhiarmada to give more emphasis to words that might be lost in the pursuit of a legato line, not to take any syllables for granted, to give different colours to the words 'saggio' (wise), 'amoroso' (loving) and 'honesto' (honest), to respect the text, breathe expressively and respond to the heartbeat of the rhythms of the accompaniment. 'There is so much beauty in the pauses and the breaths', observes Crowe.

There is a reason why bel canto style is revered and it goes beyond the basic requirement of making a beautiful sound. Constant, tiny adjustments of weight, diction and meaning are what animate this music. The smoother the melody, the more demanding of detailed attention to text and intention. In twenty-five minutes of coaching, Eunil Cho's 'O rendetemi la speme … Qui la voce', from Bellini's *I Puritani*, is transformed from glacial to gripping, a state in which the perfect cadence is not guaranteed but suspended as a possibility until the very last moment.

This is the level of work required if a singer is to be more than a pretty voice – the same of course applies to any instrument, quartet, consort or orchestra. Then there are questions of character, situation and physicality, the tricks of the trade.

Mezzo-soprano Amy Holyland is encouraged to 'square up' for a fight in *Serse*'s 'Crude furie degli orridi abissi', straddling a chair, then striding around the room as a rageful king, occupying space in a more masculine fashion.

Soprano Helena Moore is persuaded to look up at the moon in Anne Trulove's 'No word from Tom' from Stravinsky's *The Rake's Progess* ('It may be cheesy but it works', says Crowe), while Aimée Fisk is told to 'make the French sexier' in Manon's 'Suis-je gentile … Obéissons', sexiness being Manon's USP in Massenet's version of her story. 'Play with your performances', urges Crowe.

'Doing different types of repertoire is absolutely key for my enjoyment of this weird job. If I was just doing opera, or only song recitals, I'd go mad', says the tenor Allan Clayton, whose recent work has spanned recitals of Britten songs at Wigmore Hall with pianist James Baillieu, one of the youngest professors in the Academy's Piano Accompaniment Department, a staged performance of Hans Zender's orchestration of *Winterreise*, the roles of David in *Die Meistersinger von Nürnberg* at Covent Garden, Lensky in *Eugene Onegin* for Oper Frankfurt and Faust in *La Damnation de Faust*, and the creation of the title role in Brett Dean's *Hamlet* for Glyndebourne.

Mentored by Michael Dussek, a generation of accompanists, including Baillieu, Joseph Middleton, Simon Lepper and Sholto Kynoch, has grown up with the singers. 'The Academy was an ideal place for fostering this', says Clayton. 'I'd often walk straight out of an opera rehearsal on stage into a practice room with a pianist to work on Schubert, and that change of scene, musically speaking, kept me sane-ish! It meant that the transition into the professional world wasn't all that different. I just had to keep juggling the different versions of myself in front of more people.'

His breakthrough moment as a postgraduate student was during the Academy Opera production of Rameau's *Dardanus*. 'I'd never sung any French baroque music before, but thankfully the conductor, Laurence Cummings, just wanted me to sing it as I could, not perhaps as I should. On the first night we got to the aria 'Lieux funestes', and I just launched my voice at the music and didn't really care if it sounded pretty. The fusion of drama and music, and my connection to both, was intensely powerful. It felt like I was howling rather than singing. I had the same physical/emotional reaction at the end of Brett Dean's *Hamlet*.'

The countertenor Iestyn Davies, who played Ottone to Crowe's Poppea in *Agrippina*, views the postgraduate training as 'a finishing school' and 'a wake-up call'. He was part of the generation of former Cambridge choral scholars that included Clayton and Lyon. 'Singers in particular come into their own not necessarily as a result of intense tuition but rather when their personalities and technical ability align', he says. He made his Met and Glyndebourne debuts singing Handel, and enjoyed immense success in

Left: Nuccia Focile teaching
a one-to-one lesson

Opposite: Students
performing in a Musical
Theatre masterclass led by
Claude-Michel Schönberg

London and New York in Claire van Kampen's play, *Farinelli and the King*, but has also created roles in works by George Benjamin, Nico Muhly and Thomas Adès.

'It's good to remind oneself now and then that in the eighteenth century everything was new', he says. 'Singers in Handel's time were learning contemporary scores all the time. Operas were rarely revived as much as they are these days and the history of opera itself was in its infancy. So I like that modern composers are not baulking at using the sound of the countertenor in their scores and not treating the voice as a weird thing but as a serious stage instrument.'

'The truth is, it's often important to have an operatic flair in an oratorio, and it's also essential to be able to be as economic and distilled on the opera stage as it is in

a concert or a lieder performance in order to bring the audience in', says the baritone Andrew Foster-Williams, who enjoys a particular affinity with French music but is equally at home with Schubert. Projects such as the Academy Song Circle are an important experience both for the singers and the pianists on the Piano Accompaniment Course, one of the hardest careers in which to get a foothold, and one in which a pianist's finest work is often their most unobtrusive.

'In the art of being a classical singer, all the disciplines inform each other', says Foster-Williams. 'There are opera singers who feel uncomfortable in a concert because they feel exposed, with no character to hide behind. There are concert singers who can never pull off the chutzpah the opera stage requires. During my time at the Academy every

Angelika Kirchschlager giving
a vocal masterclass in the
David Josefowitz Recital Hall

student was constantly directed to embrace all of these skills in their training. I like to think we are among the most versatile out there.'

In the Susie Sainsbury Theatre technical rehearsals for Andrew Sinclair's staging of *Die Zauberflöte* are underway, watched from the back of the stalls by Production Manager Ted Murphy. In this production of Mozart's Masonic fairy tale, designed by Laura Jane Stanfield, a silhouette of three owls flies past a paper moon. There are whoops from the staff for Camilla Saba Davies, the fearless undergraduate soprano who has stepped up to sing the role of the Queen of the Night in both casts, applause for the dancing fox, hare and stag, and a reprimand from Stanfield for the members of the male chorus who are swishing their robes too enthusiastically.

When *Die Zauberflöte* opens in a few days time the focus will be on the singing and acting of the students, and on the playing of the Royal Academy Sinfonia. Principal Trumpet William Thomas and Principal Trombone James Druce both played in the Strauss *Festmusik*. The co-leader of the Sinfonia, Victoria Gill, will be leading the symphony orchestra in Sir Mark Elder's all-Berlioz programme at the end of term. What they achieve collectively will be supported not just by the conductor but by a team of professionals who rarely take a bow: carpenters, electricians, wardrobe, hair and make-up assistants, most of them regular freelancers with opera companies.

Former Head of Stage at English National Opera, now Production Manager at Opera Holland Park, Murphy has worked in opera since 1972. Stage Manager Jocelyn Bundy and Deputy Stage Manager Paul Carr come from families of theatre professionals. Theatre Technical Manager Michael 'Skip' Francis has worked in theatre from the age of

sixteen, studied Music Production and Film Composition at university in Australia, and is a full-time member of staff.

While the theatre was being built the company was itinerant. There were Academy Opera productions of Mozart's *The Marriage of Figaro* and Offenbach's *Orpheus in the Underworld* in the Hackney Empire, the cosy Frank Matcham theatre that is the London base for English Touring Opera; stagings of Kurt Weill's *Der Dreigröschenoper* and Monteverdi's *L'incoronazione di Poppea* in Shoreditch Town Hall, a regular host venue for experimental and baroque opera during the Spitalfields Festival; a production of Handel's *Alcina* in Hackney Round Chapel; and a startling Soviet Realist-style take on Rimsky-Korsakov's *Mayskaya Noch* in Ambika P3, the vast concrete vault below the University of Westminster on Marylebone Road. The Principal Trumpet in *Mayskaya Noch* was also involved in the *Venetian Extravaganza* recording.

Backstage, during the break of the first piano dress rehearsal for *Die Zauberflöte*, Francis and Murphy pick their way past the prop table – a dagger for Pamina and a basket of painted eggs for Papagena – and climb up to the electrics mezzanine and the fly floor. The silhouette of the owls is on a tab track, the serpent is a back projection, and the paper moon is shaded by a scrim of black sharkstooth gauze. If anything, this warren of metal and fabric and star cloth and cabling and switches and soldering irons and gels and gobos and bulbs is more magical than the view from the auditorium. 'It's an easy building to work in', says Francis, who will also be working on the Musical Theatre Department's upcoming showcase on the life of producer and director Hal Prince.

The Susie Sainsbury Theatre opened in 2018 with Martin Duncan's production of Jonathan Dove's opera,

Flight, and a newly commissioned fanfare by Sir Harrison Birtwistle. Reviews in the press were as admiring of the theatre as they were of the performance. Technical facilities matter. Oliver Platt, who directed the 2019 double bill of Tchaikovsky's *Iolanta* and Ravel's *L'enfant et les sortilèges*, says the Susie Sainsbury Theatre is 'a great place to work, very easy to transfer from the rehearsal room. Crucially, the staffing is amazing, with a super friendly and knowledgeable crew and technical support.' He enjoys working with students and finds it liberating creatively. 'Part of the reason you are there is the process, and not simply the end result. It can give you a freedom to experiment more than in a house which may rely more heavily on a more traditional approach. It is a good place to push the boundaries.'

From a director's point of view Platt sees the Academy Opera training as 'learning to communicate thought, through sung text. How the breath can bring utmost clarity, and how to connect the breath, the thought, the text and the notes into a dramatic whole.' In preparation he uses games and improvisation. 'Even if you then ask for something else later, it offers a choice from where you can start, rather than building from a completely blank canvas'.

There are approximately twenty-four postgraduate singers in the Opera Department, and three Fellowships for répétiteurs. The repertoire is selected to suit the vocal cohort, which may be bass- or soprano-heavy or unusually blessed with mezzos or tenors in any given year. Those who have smaller roles or who have not been cast in that term's main production get more stage time in the performance of a selection of opera scenes, singing repertoire that they are

unlikely to sing professionally in a theatre of this quality for at least another four or five years.

This term, directed by Seb Harcombe and lit by Jake Wiltshire on a spare autumnal set of blown leaves, the selection of opera scenes includes excerpts from Massenet's *Werther*, Beethoven's *Fidelio*, Williams's *Sir John in Love* and Humperdinck's *Hänsel und Gretel*. Hazel Neighbour, First Lady in the second cast of *Die Zauberflöte*, reappears as Mimì in Puccini's *La bohème*; Silja Elsabet Brynjarsdóttir, Third Lady in the first cast of *Die Zauberflöte*, reappears as Bizet's Carmen. It is a chance to explore the experience of 'holding a moment' on a stage in those arias, duets and ensembles where the action stops and the focus is on character. Among the conductors working on the scenes is Head of Conducting Sian Edwards's sole female pupil in the current intake of five students, Chloe Rooke.

Susan Bullock, now the Marjorie Thomas Visiting Professor of Singing, a title created in memory of her late teacher, left the Academy as a light coloratura soprano. As a student she played the Queen of the Night in *Die Zauberflöte*, Miss Wordsworth in Britten's *Albert Herring*, Anne Trulove in *The Rake's Progress* and the title role in Handel's *Semele*. She entered the Glyndebourne chorus, sang the role of Second Bridesmaid on tour in *The Marriage of Figaro*, then went to the Opera Studio for further training.

It was a steady progression to lyric roles such as Pamina, Gilda and Mimì, and onwards to Jenůfa, Kát'a Kabanová, Tatyana, Ellen Orford, Tosca and Cio-Cio San. 'You'd sing one thing', she says, 'and then someone would say, I hear this in your voice, and you're onto the next notch. It's slow. Very slow.' Next came the big dramatic roles, Strauss and

Wagner. Of the sopranos who preceded her at the Academy, Dame Felicity Lott gave her final recital in 2013, while Lesley Garrett was cast alongside Bullock in Iain Bell's *Jack the Ripper: The Women of Whitechapel*. Bullock stresses the importance of encouraging young singers to aim for longevity.

She is enjoying taking older roles now, mixing turns as Mrs Lovett in Sondheim's *Sweeney Todd* with the Berlin Philharmonic, with playing mothers – usually bad ones – often in operas in which she has previously played the role of a daughter. 'After eighteen different productions of *Elektra*, Klytaemnestra somehow went in by osmosis. Having played Jenůfa it's fun to play the Kostelnička. When I started in David Pountney's production of *Hansel and Gretel* I was the Sandman. Now I'm the Mother and the Witch!', she says.

'Officially I was in my prime ten years ago, doing Brünnhilde all over the world: the Met, La Scala, Covent Garden. But I feel like I'm in my prime now. Reinvention is crucial for singers because you don't ever own a role; you borrow them for a bit and then it's somebody else's turn. You've got to know when to say, thank you very much, because there's other stuff to do, and I think being aware of contemporary music is really important.'

Opera Ventures and Scottish Opera's 2017 co-production of Mark-Anthony Turnage's *Greek*, as Mum to Otterburn's Eddy, and the Edinburgh International Festival 2019 production of Missy Mazzoli's *Breaking the Waves* have been recent highlights: 'To be in the thick of something like that, with the first woman composer to be commissioned by the Met, at this point in my career, was fabulous.' The opening

'Reinvention is crucial for singers because you don't ever own a role; you borrow them for a bit and then it's somebody else's turn.'

of the Susie Sainsbury Theatre was 'a revelation' to someone who made her stage debut in the old theatre. Bullock acknowledges that some venues the students will encounter in their professional lives will be harder to sing in but 'it's nice to send them out on a cushion of confidence'.

Success does not always happen overnight, especially for singers with heavier voices such as the tenor Christopher Ventris, a celebrated Parsifal in Vienna and Bayreuth, who hit his stride in heroic and anti-heroic roles more than a decade after graduation. For the Australian soprano Helena Dix, the transition from student life to professional life was 'bloody tough'. While her lighter-voiced contemporaries eased into baroque, classical and contemporary opera,

adding weightier roles as they progressed, Dix had a voice type that 'finds itself' with time. 'I wasn't really sure what jobs to take and where they were going to take me, despite having an agent', she says. 'You have to be so disciplined and keep believing in yourself.' Now she is blossoming into repertoire as Strauss's Ariadne and Bellini's Norma, and made her Metropolitan Opera debut in 2019 as Alice Ford in Verdi's *Falstaff*.

Every Saturday, Junior Academy takes over the building. The musicians are younger but the ethos is the same. Lutenist Elizabeth Kenny, jazz pianist Kit Downes, violinist Thomas Gould, conductor Ben Glassberg, trumpeter Zoë Perkins, flautist Charlotte Ashton and many other Academy students and professors started their musical training here – as did numerous others, like Sir Andrew Davis, in the last century. This afternoon the orchestra is running through the last movement of Camille Saint-Saëns's Symphony No. 3 in C Minor, with the Sir Elton John and Ray Cooper organ singing at full tilt. Perhaps the young organist will follow alumni Simon Preston and, more recently, Peter Holder to Westminster Abbey.

Upstairs Rafael Todes, second violinist in the Allegri Quartet, is coaching students working on Beethoven's String Quartet No. 15, adjusting bowing and dynamics, separating the lines and rebuilding them, reworking small sections at half-speed, breaking the cells down then encouraging the strings to blend in consort.

Barely older than the toddlers who play sleepy bunnies between the Stradivarius and Amati instruments in the Academy Tots sessions in the museum, the youngest learners start to play the violin in groups from the age of four. From eight they might continue to Primary Academy, where Mariatu Kanneh-Mason, the youngest of the seven Kanneh-Mason siblings, is studying, and from twelve to Junior Academy proper, where Mariatu's elder sisters Aminata and Jeneba study each weekend. As Joanna MacGregor and other professors have pointed out, performers need to have experience in performing.

Parents, grandparents, siblings and teachers gather in the Duke's Hall to hear a percussion quartet play works by Adam Parnell and Jared Spears on marimba, vibraphone, glockenspiel and drums. There is a ravishing account of the first movement of Mozart's Clarinet Quintet from a clarinettist with a tone like strawberries and cream; freshwater clarity from two recorder players, a harpsichordist and cellist in a carefully paced reading of Vivaldi's Variations on La Folia; warmth and expressivity in the first movement of Dvořák's Piano Quintet from an ensemble led by Jeneba Kanneh-Mason; and a blaze of historical allusions in the UK premiere of Jon Hansen's *Climb* for brass ensemble.

Opposite: Open Academy Fellow Alice Poppleton playing in an Academy Tots session in the museum

Right: The Kanneh-Mason family on the Academy main staircase - all the Kanneh-Mason siblings attended, or still attend, Junior Academy

If Jeneba, Aminata and Mariatu follow their siblings Sheku, Braimah, Konya and Isata into the Academy, the woman behind the most pivotal performances during their studies will be Nicola Mutton. She trained as a violinist at what was then the Royal Scottish Academy of Music and Drama, moving into artistic administration with the Scottish Ensemble and the Britten Sinfonia before joining the Royal Academy of Music in 2001. She is now Director of Artistic Planning, working up to three years ahead on collaborations with the Czech Philharmonic and The Juilliard School, and programmes with visiting conductors including Marin Alsop, Robin Ticciati, Christian Thielemann and Ludovic Morlot, and members of 'the family': Semyon Bychkov (Klemperer Chair of Conducting), Sir Mark Elder (Barbirolli Chair of Conducting), Trevor Pinnock (Principal Guest Conductor, Academy Chamber Orchestra), Ryan Wigglesworth (Richard Rodney Bennett Professor of Music), Laurence Cummings (William Crotch Professor of Historical Performance), Edward Gardner (Mackerras Chair of Conducting) and John Wilson (Visiting Professor of Conducting).

'Anything that has the Academy's name on it that we do inside or outside comes through me or my team', Mutton says. This includes overseeing collaborations with The Juilliard School, from taking the Academy Baroque Orchestra on tour with Juilliard 415 and Masaaki Suzuki, and co-commissioning Sir Peter Maxwell Davies's opera, *Kommilitonen!*, to BBC Proms performances with John Adams and devising the Czech Philharmonic residencies. Some flexibility is required. In certain cohorts there might be a bulge in cellos or French horns, in which case more projects will be created for them. The easy part is working with the conductors who return every year. 'They love working with the students. It started off from them having positive experiences and good projects. We've got very good student discipline orchestrally so the projects all have a very positive feel', she says.

'You've got to catch the younger conductors before they make it really big because then you'll struggle to get them as they're really busy, but if they're alumni then, yes, they'll want to come back. The more senior ones definitely want to

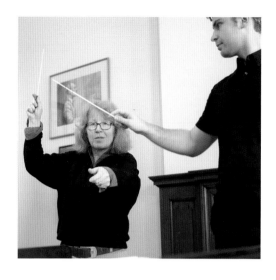

give something back. Sir Colin Davis, for example, I worked with him for many years and he never accepted a fee. It was a bottle of whisky every time and we had so much fun.'

The Haydn and Beethoven concert with the Academy Chamber Orchestra was Lorenza Borrani's second project with the students. 'She's amazing', says Mutton, 'She's joined the fold, and the concert has had over 100,000 views because Classic FM shared it on Facebook.' Livestreaming of concerts, which involves a team of five technicians, is about more than brand recognition. 'My main priority is to give the students the best possible project live', says Mutton. 'It's something we can share with a wider audience in terms of student recruitment, but it's also so that students' families

Above: Sian Edwards teaching

Below: John Adams conducting the joint orchestra of The Juilliard School and the Royal Academy of Music at the BBC Proms in 2012

Opposite: Sir Simon Rattle rehearsing the Academy Symphony Orchestra

can watch them from wherever they are in the world because we've got such an international student population. That's brilliant, but I choose the conductors and the repertoire to give the students the best possible educational experience.'

'When we did the St Matthew Passion we livestreamed it and I remember in the beginning Trevor Pinnock wasn't so keen because he thought the comments could come in while it was happening. I said, they will but you'll be conducting, you're not going to be aware of it. Actually, the comments that started to come from literally the other side of the world were coming from friends and families of the students and it was just so heart-warming.' In addition to supporting Philip Cashian in the 200 Pieces bicentenary project, Mutton will be working with Julian West in creating 200 more pieces with secondary schools pupils and 200 external concerts in hospitals, care homes and churches. 'It's utterly incredible the amount of things they do, along with all the other projects they run, but you'd never know it', she says. 'There's no fuss.'

There is a fine balance between the 'emotional honesty' that Helena Dix sought in her operatic training at the Academy and showmanship. Musical Theatre, perhaps more than any other genre, hinges on maximising the exact point at which the two meet. Backs arched, shoulders back, fingers splayed, movements drilled to perfection, voices

Edward Gardner rehearsing the
Academy Symphony Orchestra

open and immediate, the Musical Theatre students dazzle in their autumn showcase, *Hal Prince: A Life in the Theatre*.

Devised by Musical Director Daniel Bowling, Head of Musical Theatre at the Academy, and Director Matt Ryan, it is a smart and witty survey of Prince's long career as a producer and director, with seamlessly integrated numbers from *Zorba*, *Company*, *She Loves Me*, *A Doll's Life*, *A Little Night Music*, *Cabaret*, *Follies*, *Candide*, *Pacific Overtures*, *Kiss of the Spider Woman*, *Evita*, *Grind*, *On the Twentieth Century*, *Parade*, *Merrily We Roll Along*, *Sweeney Todd*, *The Phantom of the Opera* and *Show Boat*.

There are 35 members in the cast, switching seamlessly between solo numbers and ensemble pieces, speech and song, and the same number of players in the pit, more than is usual in most West End shows. In addition to strings, brass and woodwind, there is a harp, an accordion and a

Below: Royal Academy Opera production of Jonathan Dove's *Flight*

Opposite: Academy Musical Theatre Company's production of *This is the Hour*

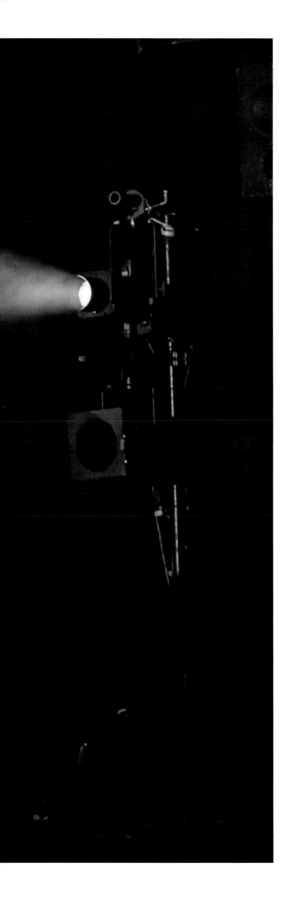

guitarist moonlighting on a mandolin and, in the number from *Zorba*, a bouzouki. The richness of the orchestral palette explains why some people say that the emphasis on this Musical Theatre course is on music.

The goosebumps are in inverse proportion to the number of props. The show is about life in the wings and on the stage, among the costume rails, in the rehearsal studios, sashaying between hits and flops. It is smoke and mirrors, vaping and vamping, sequins and sparkle, with a strong Fosse/Verdon vibe to the songs of flirtation, enchantment, heartbreak and survival.

Bowling has been in charge of Musical Theatre for four years, a department famously founded by Mary Hammond. As a former Music Director and Music Supervisor for Cameron Mackintosh, Andrew Lloyd Webber and Disney, he has worked the contacts built up over twenty-five years to tighten the connection between training and the industry, and brought in Disney-funded scholarships for under-represented communities that are likely to have experienced racism. 'I have access to the brightest and the best and I try to get them in to work with the students day in and day out. That's certainly what I've been endeavouring to do since I got here', he says.

Competition for places on the course is intense. What does he look for in auditions? 'I look for unique voices. I look for people that are open and listen and are idiosyncratic and aren't afraid. That they're brave. That they're courageous performers. That they're instinctive performers. We've got

Academy Musical Theatre
Company's production
of *The Sweet Smell
of Success*

Overleaf: Royal Academy
Opera production of Jonathan
Dove's *Flight*

'I would encourage any student to not limit themselves into thinking they are good at one thing or another. You don't know what's around the corner.'

students on the course who've got bachelor's degrees in music, and we've got students who can't read music and have no experience of notation or music theory, and oftentimes those musicians end up being the best musicians of all.'

The corridor leading to the Musical Theatre studios is littered with leg warmers and jazz shoes. The work is physically, emotionally and intellectually demanding. Delivering a spine-tingling 11 o'clock number is not enough to secure a career. 'I would love to think we've excelled at elevating the music training they receive as well as the dramatic training', says Bowling.

'With Musical Theatre they have to be equal partners. If you don't achieve that then you're really setting the students up to fail. The stress is more and more on what they bring to the table dramatically. I think we're supporting them musically in a way that no other institution is able to, and we've been able to offer them incredible training dramatically. That's something I've really focused on and I think the evidence is that we're doing the right job on that front from the sheer number of students who are employed after the course.'

Headline Musical Theatre alumni include Hadley Fraser, Rachel Tucker, Paige Smallwood, Fra Fee, Sam Oladeinde, Stephenson Ardern-Sodje and Shona White. Alongside the department's company of singer-actors, some from a drama background, some classically trained, Bowling trains a handful of musical directors. 'Virtually every show in the West End has one of our graduates', he says. 'Every single one of our MDs has walked straight into really amazing opportunities and I'm very proud of that. We're doing it at a whole different level to anyone else out there. Obviously it's very competitive. We only accept three students a year, and we have amazing

people teaching them, and we couldn't run the course without them. They're fully immersed in it and they come out the other side of the course as very different musicians.'

In *The Oxford Handbook of Opera*, essayist Derek B. Scott refers to six vocal qualities specific to the musical, each determined by the position of the larynx. Somewhat alarmingly, the term 'belt' is defined as 'lifted larynx – as about to scream'. Alumnus Fra Fee has vivid memories of the first time his vocal teacher unlocked his 'belt'. 'Until that point, I was very much a lyric tenor, having spent most of my young life singing lieder and opera', he says.

'There was inevitably a sense of separation between the slightly rebellious, somewhat chaotic Musical Theatre troupe with their improvisation and tap shoes and the diligence and concentration of the rest of the school, but I loved making my way through the rehearsal rooms to the MT wing, hearing cellos and French horns practising of a morning.' Musical Theatre alumna Kate Marlais, recently resident composer at the Lyric Theatre, Hammersmith, would often go into the main building to hear the vocal recitals.

'Being an MT student in a core classical institution was nothing but inspiring', she says. 'It certainly kept my love of classical music alive, with so much talent to feed off for my postgraduate year.' She joined the course as a classical soprano with a knack for comedy and acting. 'With coaching, encouragement and opportunity, I was able to find new vocal qualities in my voice and discover new sounds I didn't know I could produce, that would bring something new to my performances, which was really exciting and gave me many more options to look into when stepping out into the "real world".'

When Fee arrived all he wanted to do was to play Marius in *Les Misérables* on stage: 'A lovely dream, of course, but once that's fulfilled, what then?' He regards the variety of work he has done from Sondheim to Shakespeare to Jez Butterworth's *The Ferryman* and the film of *Les Misérables* as a gift. 'I would encourage any student to not limit themselves into thinking they are good at one thing or another. You don't know what's around the corner. Keep your options open because we're all so full of potential.'

Kathryn Adamson, Librarian, has worked at the Academy since 1990. Together with Gabrielle Gale, she seeks out relevant items from the special collections of scores, manuscripts and letters for the temporary exhibitions in the museum. She is quietly spoken, practical, methodical and also idealistic. 'With some scores, you wouldn't want them open on the same page for too long. You wouldn't put something on permanent exhibition where the binding could get damaged. But apart from that, pretty much

Overleaf: Musical Theatre students and Matt Lucas (front row, second from right) performing a scene from *Les Misérables*

everything is up for grabs. The whole reason we have a museum is to be able to display all these wonderful things that we've had for years and years but never had the means to exhibit them. That's why we do it, and I just love the fact that things are being used.'

Detective work appeals to her, drawing connections across countries and through history: tracing the relationships behind the score of *A Midsummer Night's Dream* that was given to Sir George Smart by Mendelssohn, and the composer's connection with Sir William Sterndale Bennett; investigating the careers of long-dead students and teachers through the comparison of minute books and report cards; and poring over yellowed letters in albums of music. 'It always surprises me that people who wrote all the time didn't have much nicer handwriting', she says. 'Actually, I think that because people wrote all the time, everybody was much better at deciphering different hands.'

Adamson has to decide which books and scores to keep, and which to remove. This morning she has been 'de-duplicating' a pile of songs behind her desk. 'There's a difference between dated and classic', she points out. 'It was easier with the book room because there you've got a choice between Helmholtz, a classic on acoustics, and somebody trying to explain Helmholtz in a 1930s' style. When you have students whose first language is not English, reading outdated language is not going to help and could be very misleading.'

Today there are 114,194 items in the lending library. Tomorrow there could be more or less, depending on gifts and disposals. Adamson's focus, however, is on trying to link the collections with the teaching that is going on. 'A loan collection should always be a working collection and should be both immediately useful to the students and give them a

bit more breadth to explore.' She is particularly pleased when a teacher asks for a volume of music and she is able to provide an original historical publication rather than a facsimile.

Cataloguing the special collections, including the Menuhin, Mackerras, Munrow, Wood, Klemperer and Robert Spencer collections, and reproducing them for online access, is an ongoing project. The earliest item found so far is a letter from a lute teacher to his pupil's master, dating from the mid-fifteenth century. There are many important items: Joah Bates's letter of 16 July 1784 to Charles Burney; a manuscript copy of Purcell's *The Fairy Queen*; and Handel's setting of the Gloria for soprano and strings, which was discovered as recently as 2000. There are rarities such as two leaves from James Rowbotham's 1569 guide to playing and tuning the guitar, which had been discovered as endpapers in a volume of *Certain Godly Sermons Preached by Hugh Latymer*. Then there are personal favourites, among them Thomas Mace's copy of Thomas Morley's *A Plaine and Easie Introduction to Practicall Musicke*, and a set of partbooks from William Byrd and Thomas Tallis's *Cantiones Sacrae* from 1575.

'It's not unique but it is a lovely thing, and it's an important slice of music publishing history', says Adamson. What is unique about the Discant partbook is that it is wrapped in an illuminated missal from the 1400s. 'It's vellum, that cover; and I like that it was surplus to requirements, so they just reused it.' In the afternoon she takes it to Patrick Russill's quintet of MA students on the Choral Conducting course, happily one soprano, one alto, one tenor, a baritone and a bass.

'It's pre-Reformation music looking after post-Reformation music', says Russill, examining the missal. 'Can we smell this?' They bend in to inhale the scent of pages that were printed in Blackfriars when Tallis was seventy and Byrd thirty-five. The pages smell of cinders and woodsmoke. Tentatively, with Adamson joining in on the alto line, they begin to sing Tallis's motet, 'O nata lux de lumine', stopping to discuss form (a sarabande) and performance conventions long since replaced by changes in notation.

A dozen boxes are stacked against the wall of Philip Cashian's office. In them are piles of orchestral scores and books, toys and trinkets, from the estate of the Academy's much-loved former teacher, the conductor and composer Oliver Knussen, who died in 2018. In one box there is a stuffed toy of Max, the anti-hero of Knussen's operatic adaptation of Maurice Sendak's children's story, *Where the Wild Things Are*. In another, there is a tiny, wooden bird in a box, a Japanese cuckoo. When you press the bottom of the box, it sings. This bird was the inspiration for one of Knussen's last compositions, 'O Hototogisu', for soprano, flute and ensemble.

To Cashian, becoming a composer seemed 'a natural thing to be'. As Head of Composition at the Royal Academy of Music, he enjoys what he says is a perfect combination of intensive teaching and composing his own music. 'I'd hate to be at home by myself all the time composing. I'd just go mad', he says. All of the composition staff are freelance composers and the job is immensely creative, from programming to planning performances. Cashian is currently writing a piece for George Fu, as part of a programme of newly composed piano Études by Robert Saxton, Mark-Anthony Turnage and nine Masters students, and is working with Nicola Mutton on the 200 Pieces project, which was initially inspired by Luciano Berio's Sequenzas.

Cashian's colleague, David Sawer, is overseeing a new collaboration with the Opera Department, putting six student composers together with six librettists to write five-minute duos with piano accompaniment, from which three will be chosen to be developed into semi-staged ten-minute scenes with ensemble. 'It used to be a bit of a struggle to get the instrumentalists and singers to work with the composers but now it's absolutely not a problem at all', he says. 'Performers are coming to the composers and asking to work on projects, asking them for pieces and to collaborate, so the age-old problem has completely vanished.'

Every piece that is written in the department is performed. In the Composers' Platform Concert in the David Josefowitz Recital Hall there are works by undergraduates Electra Perivolaris, Rebecca Farthing, Margarida Gonçalves, Antonino Abate and Iason Maroulis, which range from post-Romantic miniatures for violin and piano to an eight-part a cappella setting of an Alice Oswald poem and a Berioesque showpiece for unaccompanied clarinet.

Cashian is proud of the stylistic diversity. 'It's not something we can actively try to encourage, because the students write what they write, but I think it's a strength and I know all the staff feel the same. There's a huge range in every single concert and people are always commenting on how different the writing is. I think it's really healthy. There's no house style. That would be dreadful.' In their first year of studies, the composers are 'fast-tracked' through a course of techniques of composition that runs from the late nineteenth century to the present day, via serialism and spectralism.

The Danish composer Hans Abrahamsen visits for three days each term, giving seminars and one-to-one lessons

> The earliest item found so far is a letter from a lute teacher to his pupil's master, dating from the mid-fifteenth century.

with eighteen students. Knussen conducted Abrahamsen's first piece, back in the 1980s, and both men were championed by the late Hans Werner Henze, one of the first composers to be featured in the Academy's Composer Festivals. More recent visiting composers include Magnus Lindberg, Andrew Norman, Anna Thorvaldsdottir, Georg Friedrich Haas and, of course, alumnus Sir Harrison Birtwistle.

Like Cashian, Abrahamsen views the diversity of voices as a healthy thing. 'In the 1960s you had to teach in one voice', he says. 'In some places it was almost that you had to write in that way to be a "modern composer". That has changed. In Denmark we have always had the tradition of developing the different voices of the different composers, somehow to take the starting point from them. If it's something that I don't like, then it's my limitation.'

'Style is something that students shouldn't really think about', says Cashian. 'I think it's a by-product of writing music. They're young and they should just be trying everything. Do one thing and then do the opposite. Be as open-minded as possible.' Creativity, he says, can be fostered and facilitated but not taught. 'You can train people to develop their technical skills and you can expose them to all sorts of different situations but ultimately the creativity is either there or it's not.'

With the acquisition of two 3D projectors in the Creative Technology Suite, some composition Masters students have been experimenting with audiovisual installations and holograms, while their peers are writing string quartets and solo piano pieces. 'It's all connected and it's all related and the broader it is the better', says Cashian. 'All that matters is the quality of what they're doing and how we make sure that the students are writing what they really want to write and doing it to the highest possible standard. As a composer I think you have to push and push and push what you want to do to the absolute maximum.'

The centrepiece of Abrahamsen's visit this term is a performance by the Academy Manson Ensemble, directed by the conductor, composer and pianist, Ryan Wigglesworth. Abrahamsen's signature glittering textures, haunting drones and shivering tempi are made beautifully clear in the ensemble's performances of *Märchenbilder*,

Winternacht and *Wald*. These frozen landscapes are contrasted with the world premiere of PhD student Joseph Howard's *Pink Tons* for flute, piano, clarinet, violin, horn, cello and trumpet. It is a substantial, confident work, frosted with pitchless breaths, warmed by flecks of lyricism and a preternaturally poised performance.

Augusta Read Thomas, Philip Venables, Benjamin Wallfisch, Dominic Lewis, Max Richter, Luke Bedford and Freya Waley-Cohen are among the most prominent younger composers to have studied in the department. Waley-Cohen remembers coming to the Academy for a consultation lesson with Simon Bainbridge. 'When I left, I couldn't wait to go home and write music', she says. As a student, it was the first time that she had been able to focus solely on composition instead of fitting it around other work. 'It gave me a feeling of restless, buzzy energy. My main memory of that time is that energy, and feeling that excitement, especially when I was walking towards the building.'

She experimented during her Masters, trying out different ideas with the support of Bainbridge and Cashian. The point at which things clicked was just as she had started her PhD studies with Knussen. 'His belief in my music and excitement about my ideas allowed me the self-belief to take this step and find out what I had to say, and more importantly, to keep asking myself that question and pushing the ideas further with each piece.' She has since written pieces for the

The Principal's office with
Wagner's music stand and
Mozart's table

'His belief in my music
and excitement about
my ideas allowed
me the self-belief to
take this step and find
out what I had to say,
and to keep… pushing
the ideas further
with each piece.'

Los Angeles Philharmonic, the BBC Proms, The Hermes Experiment and the Aldeburgh Festival.

'Without sounding too cheesy, it did slightly change my life', says Venables, whose second opera, *Denis & Katya*, is about to tour the UK after its Philadelphia premiere. He studied Natural Sciences at university and had plenty of passion and originality in his writing but little formal musical education. 'Phil Cashian is a very practical, down-to-earth teacher and composer, which was exactly what I needed at that stage. I'd had no training and he gave me a really good technical grounding, and introduced me to lots of music. I was playing catch-up with all these people who had done music degrees or had studied composition as undergraduates, and they just threw loads of practical projects at me.'

'It was intense, intense, intense writing, kind of vomiting out loads of pieces in a way that I would never dream of doing now. I would bring sketches for a piece when I was stuck and he would give me five different approaches I could take to whatever problem it was. Because it was so breakneck, I didn't really have time to sit and think about aesthetics or what I really wanted to do with my life. That came afterwards.'

Through the course of five years of professional development work as a young composer, Venables absorbed what he had learned with Cashian and found a way to reconnect to the 'quite rhythmic, maybe a bit naïve, lots of oompf' voice he had as a teenager. His first opera, an adaptation of Sarah Kane's play, *4.48 Psychosis*, won the 2017 Royal Philharmonic Society Award for Large-Scale Compositions and was nominated for an Olivier Award.

In the first session of the Conducting Department Open Day the prospective students experiment with conducting a two-piano arrangement of Beethoven's *Eroica Symphony*. They are mentored by conductor Sian Edwards, head of the department, and her five students, Roc Fargas i Castells, Henry Kennedy, Thomas Fetherstonhaugh, Edward Liebrecht and Chloe Rooke, for whom the experience of teaching is itself a learning process. Coordinating two pianists, with one grand piano to the right of the podium and one to the left, is harder than it might seem, especially when those pianists have been instructed to follow each conductor's movements exactly, whether they lose or gain speed or miscue an entry.

Consider the difficulty of the old trick of rubbing one's tummy while patting one's head, then imagine what it

Oliver Knussen leading a
workshop in the Duke's Hall

would be like if the strings were following one movement and the brass were following the other. If both hands are doing the same thing, in mirror image, then the expressive and stylistic possibilities are halved. Conductors are not human metronomes.

The feedback is highly detailed: a combination of examining the orchestral score and differentiating successive sforzando markings, allowing space for the woodwind lines to breathe, being mindful of a pivotal phrase in the cello part, learning how to use both arms and hands to shape dynamics and hold tempi, and connecting the very tip of the baton to the sound. In the second session, the prospective students are joined by an ad hoc orchestra of undergraduates, alternating excerpts from the Beethoven with movements from Stravinsky's neoclassical ballet, *Pulcinella*. Patiently, Edwards reiterates the importance of listening more thoroughly than from the top down, of keeping physical gestures succinct and 'receiving' the sound.

Sir Simon Rattle, Susanna Mälkki, Ilan Volkov, Odaline de la Martinez, David Robertson, Ludovic Morlot, Mark Wigglesworth, Richard Farnes, Valentina Peleggi and Edward Gardner all trained at the Academy. Since Edwards took over the department in 2013, repurposing a three-year repertoire-based course into what she describes as a two-year, technique-based 'lily pad', alumni have included the young conductors Jonathon Heyward, Ray Chan, Ben

Paul Carr (Deputy Stage Manager), takis (designer) and Olivia Fuchs (Director) preparing for the Royal Academy Opera production of Handel's *Semele* in the Susie Sainsbury Theatre

Overleaf: Academy Musical Theatre Company's production of *The Sweet Smell of Success*

Glassberg, Johann Von Stuckenbruck, Joel Sandelson, Bertie Baigent, Eli Brown and Adam Hickox. Between them they have worked with Glyndebourne, English National Opera, the Hallé, the Colorado Symphony, the BBC Scottish Symphony Orchestra, the Auckland Philharmonia and the Hong Kong Sinfonietta since leaving, and in projects of their own devising in collaboration with visual artists. 'Everyone goes at different speeds', says Edwards.

Douglas Boyd was in his forties and an established solo oboist before he turned to conducting, inspired by twenty-one years of watching and working with Claudio Abbado and Bernard Haitink with the Chamber Orchestra of Europe. He never had any formal training, 'just lots of one-to-one conversations – were they lessons? – with some wonderful conductors.' Boyd is glad that he waited before changing direction. Morlot, who credits the late Sir Colin Davis as his greatest musical inspiration, encouraging him to look at art and literature to find answers to questions of colour and narrative in orchestral scores, remembers struggling as a student 'to erase that feeling of self-consciousness' and build his voice as an artist.

'This fear of being judged constantly ends up being unhelpful and unhealthy for both the orchestra and the conductor', says Morlot. It is also a contributory factor in a still-prevalent gender imbalance on the podium, as Edwards acknowledges. 'It's to do with occupying space. It's also to do with assumptions of authority', she says. 'I think there are real dissonances for women that are not necessarily there for men. I think the women that are coming to it are coming to it a bit later. And I think women feel they've got to be more qualified and more secure in themselves before they just give it a go.'

Self-consciousness can be a blessing as well as a curse when so much of a conductor's work is expressed without words, and when a large part of the training is based on analysing videos of one's movements and gestures and practising in front of a mirror. Since Mirga Gražinytė-Tyla's appointment to the City of Birmingham Symphony Orchestra more young women have applied to join conducting courses at every level. 'She's showing that you can be "feminine", if you like, on the platform, that you can be creative and that it really works. So that's definitely helping', says Edwards. In the field of choral conducting, where Gražinytė-Tyla began her training, the numbers are almost equal. Still there is often a gap between male applicants who have been conducting their own groups since their mid-teens and female applicants who have been slower to put themselves forward when they come to audition for Edwards's course.

'It's frustrating to me because I can't do positive discrimination', says Edwards. 'I've only got five people in the whole programme, three first years and two second years, and I don't think the women would want me to do that.' Two of the prospective students at the Open Day are members of the Sorrell Women's Conducting Programme, a project Edwards set up with the Cristiana Falcone Sorrell Foundation to address that difference in confidence and practical experience. Last year there were five applicants for every place on a scheme that runs across three intensive weekends, ending with an orchestra or ensemble, filming everything and discussing every aspect of the work, with Gardner as a mentor. This year sixty-nine people applied for the two or three places on the conducting course proper.

Edwards's own route into conducting was unconventional for a woman of her age: 'I wasn't a very girly girl, so I didn't really care what other people thought of me so much.' She went to the Royal Northern College of Music as a French horn player, having had experience conducting sectional rehearsals of her local youth orchestra and with ensembles of groups of friends. She took conducting lessons in London, then won a scholarship to a summer school with the Estonian conductor Neeme Järvi. 'I remember saying to him, "how do I conduct like you?" And he said, "you have to study in Leningrad".'

It was 1983 and relations between the UK and the Soviet Union were poor. An exchange scheme place was arranged with funding from the British Council and Edwards arrived, unable to speak the language. At first she was assigned to the class of Arvīds Jansons, Mariss Jansons's father. Soon she realised that she wanted to study with Ilya Musin,

Head of Conducting at Leningrad Conservatory. A student from Kazakhstan coached her for her audition with Musin. He accepted her, and she began ten months of study as his first Western student. She won the Leeds Conducting Competition, then returned for a further year with Musin. When she came back to the UK, people began to ask for lessons with her.

The Russian School centres on the idea that the sound is in your hands, that you might lift it with the tip of the baton or crush it. Edwards quotes Musin: 'My delicate chickens! I pick up a chick! I pick up a strawberry!' She agrees with Morlot that only so much can be taught in a conservatoire but sees the two-year course as an opportunity to 'put your conducting under the microscope'. The first professional steps may be difficult but 'you really sort out your hands and learn work in a much deeper, thorough and interesting way than you've ever done before. You also then splice what you're doing with your hands with what you're imagining the sound to be, the tempo and everything else.'

Ben Glassberg began working as an assistant conductor at Glyndebourne while he was still studying with Edwards, and was the youngest conductor to debut at the Festival. He is currently Principal Conductor of Glyndebourne on Tour, and has been appointed as Music Director of Opéra de Rouen Normandie. Glassberg had taken conducting lessons for six years when he decided he needed a fresh pair of eyes, and was in Edwards's second intake. 'Everyone I spoke to said that she was the best. She's just so forensic in the way that she approaches technique and she has a very clear methodology', he says. He was also attracted to the idea of the connection to the sound that Edwards had learned

Self-consciousness
can be a blessing
as well as a curse
when so much
of a conductor's
work is expressed
without words.

from Musin. The conductor who inspired him to think about opera was another Academy alumnus, Mark Wigglesworth. As a student Glassberg conducted opera scenes and observed visiting conductors including Robin Ticciati, Gardner, Bychkov and Elder.

Edwards's students are sitting in the Duke's Hall as Sir Mark Elder takes the Academy Symphony Orchestra through the last day of rehearsals for their end of term concert of Berlioz's Overture to *Les francs-juges*, 'March to the Scaffold', 'March of the Pilgrims' and *King Lear* Overture. Each of them has prepared part of the programme with Edwards and conducted the orchestra prior to Elder's arrival. Now they are observing, scores in their laps, as Elder fine-tunes a passage from *Harold en Italie*. An exacting conductor with professional players, he is equally exacting with the student orchestra.

'Walk away! Walk away! Whisper!', urges Elder, hushing the tutti strings as viola soloist Erik Fauss traces the cross-string passages. 'One hundred per cent concentration! After all that fruitiness we've got to make the audience think

Semyon Bychkov rehearsing the
Academy Symphony Orchestra

171

Alumnae Dame Evelyn Glennie,
Lesley Garrett and Dame Felicity
Lott with former Principal
Sir Curtis Price and Her Majesty
the Queen at the 2007 royal visit

we're back to the beginning.' Turneresque clouds of colour roll into view and recede as Anwen Thomas's harp sounds a single, starlit note. 'Don't push! Listen! Let it come to rest! Now coffee! It's going to be fine.' As the players disperse, Elder gives notes to the leader of the orchestra, Victoria Gill, then leaves the podium and talks to the student conductors.

The violin professor Philippe Honoré describes the role of a leader as 'a link between the orchestra and the conductor'. What is striking about Gill is how self-contained she is. As Honoré says, it is a job in which you use all of your senses, 'you have to obviously be on top of the music but you're looking around constantly at the conductor, your co-principals and using your ears'. Over the course of the morning the scent of mince pies creeps in from the foyer. The Christmas tree has been decorated and some brass players have returned wearing paper party hats.

Elder's injunctions continue: 'Louder! Not you!', 'Don't be late! Don't be early! Perfect!', 'Let it vibrate! Have the sound ready in your ear before you play it!' All the rheum and rage

and regret of Berlioz's Lear begin to settle into the sound. 'Don't worry! I'll be with you! Beautiful!', he says to the oboist Ignacio Cano Raboso. 'More life! More imagination! Speak it!', to the cellos. 'Not mysterious enough!', to the bassoonist, Patrick Bolton, as they begin the 'March to the Scaffold'. 'Are those mince pies any good? Save me one!'

Elder, who six months earlier conducted David Butt Philip in *La Damnation de Faust* with the Hallé, explains Berlioz beautifully. He stops the players mid-phrase to expand on the bizarreness of the 'March to the Scaffold', the malevolence, the vulgarity, the righteous fury, the dirt. 'It's not opéra comique!' He talks to them about the execution of Anne Boleyn in the television adaptation of Hilary Mantel's *Wolf Hall*, the strike of the blade. Some students giggle nervously. Some of them look queasy. The point has been made: this pizzicato passage must sound like the roll of a severed head. In the lullaby caress of *Les francs-juges* he reminds the cello section to watch Gill. 'She may be wrong. I don't care. You need to be with her!'

Opposite: Christian Thielemann
rehearsing the Academy Symphony
Orchestra in the Duke's Hall

These hours, and the performance that follows them, are where this term's work comes together. In the fearlessness of the brass players, with Holly Clark on cornet; the close blending of the woodwind, led by Jagoda Krzemińska, Raboso, James Gilbert and Bolton; the refinement of the strings. Jared Prokop, last seen in Graham Mitchell's masterclass, is leading the double basses. Quentin Broyart, timpanist in the *Festmusik*, and Andrea Dominguez de Dios, percussionist in the Musical Theatre showcase and the Manson Ensemble, are here. So is Robyn Blair, horn player in *Die Zauberflöte*.

The conducting students are not the only people who have been observing Elder's rehearsal. In the control room on the first floor, a few minutes before the livestreamed concert is about to begin, Oliver Glynn is testing the joystick with which he will switch between six cameras. There are twenty-three microphones and spot mics to give a natural perspective to the sound, which will be balanced by Andrew Lang from his mixing desk in the back of the Duke's Hall.

Leo Loock is score reader and shot caller today. Daniel Erlich, the live switcher, has planned the whole production, a task that takes between thirty and forty hours. His orchestral scores are marked up with blue and red notes of shot changes. A composer and conductor, he has identified points in the music where he can 'guide people's ears with their eyes'. Watched by David Gleeson, Head of Recording at the Royal Academy of Music since 2013, the team only resorts to improvising when something goes wrong. In the livestream of Borrani's performance with the Academy Chamber Orchestra, a camera on the balcony was kicked and went offline.

'A43, D41, A43, E47, C49, D41, F45', calls Loock as the concert starts. 'He's going really maestoso,' says Erlich, as Elder sets a broad and determined pulse, 'which means the next bit is going to be really f****** fast! Come on, horns!' The tempo changes to a blistering presto. There are close-ups on the trombones, cellos and basses, flutes and clarinets, the speed of the changes reflecting the structure of the score. '500 watches so far on Facebook', says Gleeson. 'Très bien', says Loock. 'My bad! We're good!', as a hiccup is averted. He and Erlich are both conducting along with Elder now, and the shots are sweetly in step with the music. As the Facebook viewing figures rise to 615, then rocket to 19,000, then 53,000, the severed head drops to the floor in 'March to the Scaffold'.

It is the fourth day of auditions for the 2020 intake. Jack Liebeck will be hearing twenty violinists today, sending those he and his fellow panel members are particularly interested in to the David Josefowitz Recital Hall, where Principal Jonathan Freeman-Attwood, the Deputy Principal or Dean and the relevant head of department will listen to potential students put forward to the Principal's Audition. 'We try and make it a welcoming experience. Because it is a positive place', he says. 'The people that work at the front desk, some of them have been here since I was a teenager. They remember everyone's name. The people that work in the canteen – Mary at the till has been here since I was an undergraduate.'

Andrew Foster-Williams, who was awarded a full scholarship when he auditioned, remembers being sent down to the David Josefowitz Recital Hall. One of the questions he was asked was why he was applying to only

The tempo changes to a blistering presto. There are close-ups on the trombones, cellos and basses, flutes and clarinets, the speed of the changes reflecting the structure of the score.

two conservatoires. 'I'll never forget the look on Jonathan's face when I told them, in a broad Wigan accent, that it was because it was £50 a pop to audition and I could only afford to do two! In my practical Lancashire brain I'd assessed that if I didn't get into a conservatoire after two auditions I obviously wasn't talented enough. I had a great time at the Academy and, my god, it was a learning curve. I could have missed out on what has been an absolutely fascinating life for the cost of a meal for two.'

This afternoon Freeman-Attwood and his deputy Tim Jones hear three violinists of distinctly different tone and style, an already highly trained lutenist with a Van Halen approach to Kapsberger, a learner-driver singer with a limousine-sized voice, a flautist whose Carl Philippe Emanuel Bach sparkles with humour, and a shy seventeen-year-old pianist from Poland whose performance of Bach's *Chromatic Fantasia and Fugue* is so intensely imagined that everyone is left speechless. There are questions about ambitions, preference of individual teachers, particular areas of interest in terms of repertoire, and about financial need.

The atmosphere is positive but the pressure is on. In the newly created role of Dean of Students, one of Elizabeth Kenny's aims is to simplify the bursary applications. It is a pleasingly straightforward step in a wider and more complex project to increase access to the education that the Academy can provide. Her remit runs from working with Julian West to develop more projects to link Open Academy to Junior Academy, to collaborating with Mark David on a scheme for young brass players in Cornwall. The Musical Theatre Department's Disney scholarships are a

Opposite and right: Recording engineer Oliver Glynn and Head of Recording David Gleeson in the studio recording a performance taking place in the Angela Burgess Recital Hall

wonderful thing but more work needs to be done to diversify the intake across departments by supporting learning at a pre-conservatoire level, as the Sorrell Women's Conducting Programme does.

Black, Asian, mixed-heritage and minority ethnic students have a long history at the Academy, as evidenced in the photographs from 1919 hanging on the wall outside the library. As Kenny points out, the institution has to be alert to a change of paradigm. 'It's not just doing it because you have a sense of social justice or you want to be nice', she says. 'It's actually that that's where the future of music is going to be, in giving yourself access to as wide a range of ideas as possible. You don't want people who think the same because they look the same.'

International from its foundation, the Royal Academy of Music now needs to fight to preserve that spirit, to continue to find ways to bring out the best from candidates from all over the world, the players and singers and composers who experiment with different styles, the new technologies and the ancient pigments and partbooks. As George Caird says, 'The age-old principle that a musician apprenticed themselves to a great teacher is one that has lived on through all the institutionalising that has gone on since the Paris Conservatoire was founded in 1794. This is because musicians know that they will only learn their art from the real thing.'

'Musicians know
that they will only
learn their art
from the real thing.'

Head of Vocal Studies Kate
Paterson giving a masterclass

Overleaf: Academy Musical
Theatre Company's production
of *The Sweet Smell of Success*

EPILOGUE

It is just under a year since the Academy Symphonic Brass Ensemble played its programme of Gabrieli, Henze and Strauss in the Duke's Hall. It is enrolment week at the Academy and a tepee has been erected outside the building for the 2020 intake of new students. Second-year undergraduate Holly Clark, who opened last year's concert as a fresher, is practising downstairs. So is Zoë Perkins, who graduated with the top mark of the fourth-year undergraduate trumpet final recitals this summer, and has returned to the Academy for her postgraduate studies.

The building has been made Covid-secure, with one-way systems, perspex screens, socially distanced seating and a strict capacity on any day, but the music has not stopped. Ian Ritchie's new spaces are vital to what has become the 'new normal'. A baroque string orchestra has been playing in the Angela Burgess Recital Hall. The Susie Sainsbury Theatre is being made ready for Academy Opera's forthcoming production of Britten's *A Midsummer Night's Dream*, in which the cast will use the stage and all areas of the auditorium as a performance space.

Composer workshops have moved into the Duke's Hall. The recording technology is being used as never before: David Gleeson (Head of Recording) and his team are preparing to livestream sixty-one concerts this term, beginning with the Academy Big Band and the great saxophonist Stan Sulzmann. The Open Days, too, have moved online and in each session of questions and answers with students and professors there comes a point when prospective applicants ask about the effect of coronavirus. 'Lockdown hasn't stopped the Academy', says Jay Worley, a student in the Musical Theatre Company.

Six months after the UK went into lockdown to combat the spread of Covid-19, the students and alumni of the Academy have proved resilient. In August Aaron Akugbo, who played first trumpet in Strauss's *Festmusik der Stadt Wien*, joined the brass section of the London Symphony Orchestra in its BBC Proms performance of Gabrieli's Canzon septimi et octavi toni à 12 and Canzon noni toni à 12 under alumnus Sir Simon Rattle. Flautist Charlotte Ashton played in two concerts of this drastically revised Proms season, performed and broadcast live but without an audience on-site: first with the BBC Scottish Symphony Orchestra at Glasgow City Halls, then with the Philharmonia Orchestra at the Royal Albert Hall in a programme that included a performance of Shostakovich's Piano Concerto No. 1 with pianist Benjamin Grosvenor and trumpeter-alum Jason Evans.

The world's largest music festival shrank in size and scope this year, as though to warn us of what we might lose if we do not support the arts vigorously. The emphasis was local: Isata and Sheku Kanneh-Mason played a recital of Beethoven and Samuel Barber; tenor Allan Clayton sang Britten's *Nocturne* with the BBC Philharmonic in Salford; clarinettist Timothy Orpen, oboist Tom Barber and trombonist Matthew Gee played Beethoven's Seventh Symphony with Aurora Orchestra, the ensemble they co-founded as students. Tentatively, and in the knowledge that restrictions on live performance may be reimposed should the infection rate rise again, musical life, an exchange of energy between artist and audience that is not easily transferable to digital media, has resumed in time for the new academic year. At Garsington Douglas Boyd is

Melanie Ragge, Professor of Oboe in the Woodwind Department, teaching from home

conducting a semi-staged version of Beethoven's *Fidelio* to a small audience. There are concerts with reduced audiences at Saffron Hall, in Saffron Walden, Essex, and Wigmore Hall, and, while the weather holds, in parks and gardens across the country.

From artists to administrators, students to staff, most musicians will recall where they were when the coronavirus pandemic ceased to be the subject of harrowing news reports from Lombardy and Catalonia and became a present threat. On 15 March 2020 the LSO played a concert of music by Vaughan Williams and Britten under Antonio Pappano. By the interval, it was apparent that this would be the last public concert in the Barbican for the foreseeable future. Clayton was in rehearsal for the Royal Opera's new production of Janáček's *Jenůfa* that week. Within days, the opening of that production and future engagements in New York, Amsterdam and Aldeburgh had been postponed. Summer seasons and festivals were pulled. Orchestral tours, a vital and lucrative activity, were cancelled. The financial impact was incalculable.

The Academy locked down one week before the end of the spring term. A Response Fund was launched by the Principal, Jonathan Freeman-Attwood, with a major seed donation from Dr Matthias von der Tann. More than £300,000 was raised in short order to assist students who needed to fly home, were worried about where to store their belongings, had no access to instruments, had poor Wi-Fi or computer equipment, or were struggling to pay their rent without income from singing in churches, playing in concerts and sessions, working in box offices or waiting in restaurants.

For established professional musicians, the vast majority of them freelancers, the sudden cancellation of paid projects,

Most musicians will recall where they were when the coronavirus pandemic ceased to be the subject of harrowing news reports from Lombardy and Catalonia and became a present threat.

in some cases stretching well into 2021, was terrifying. Many did not qualify for the government's Self-Employment Income Support Scheme that gave grants of 80 per cent, then 70 per cent of typical profit across each three-month period without work. A flurry of digital activity and broadcasts of previously recorded performances from the world's leading orchestras and opera houses over April, May and June did not put food on the table. Theatres and concert venues announced they were entering redundancy consultations. The huge unseen family of lighting engineers, stage managers and assistant stage managers, set designers and builders, and arts administrators who support live performance were without work or aid. The discourse became ugly.

On the Continent, where the funding model for the arts is very different, where handsome state subsidies are a matter of course, and where, in the case of some countries, the infection rate and death toll from the virus were far lower, theatres and concert halls gradually reopened. While the LSO was mothballed, streaming socially distanced chamber music from LSO St Luke's, Rattle conducted symphonic programmes in Munich and Prague. Crude comparisons were drawn between Vienna and London, as though the local silence was a result of a lack of will or pluck on the part of Britain's musicians instead of a response to volatile infection rates, vague or contradictory safety guidelines, and a performance economy historically dependent on near-capacity ticket sales and profitable ancillary retail and hospitality outlets.

Only in July, after several weeks of musical guerrilla activity by impromptu groups of singers and instrumentalists, were the restrictions on outdoor performances lifted officially. In August Clayton joined the cast for Glyndebourne's al fresco adaptation of an Offenbach operetta, *In the Market for Love*. The Salzburg Festival went ahead, and proudly reported no infections among its audiences. Edinburgh and Aix-en-Provence did not. In Madrid, where opera had returned to the stage with 2-metre gaps between singers, a performance of Verdi's *Un ballo in maschera* was halted when a section of the audience protested that social-distancing guidelines were not being observed in their seats.

In Glasgow, Scottish Opera presented Puccini's *La bohème* in its car park, and filmed Janáček's chamber opera, *The Diary of One Who Disappeared*, for broadcast, with Ed Lyon as the young man besotted by a mysterious woman. The pubs had reopened but the Royal Opera House, the Barbican and the Royal Festival Hall in London remained closed, seemingly too large to cater for reduced audiences. In Westminster, Rishi Sunak, Chancellor of the Exchequer, stated that the British arts industry, though vastly more profitable than agriculture, and internationally renowned, was not economically viable. The implication that many thousands of highly talented and hard-working creative practitioners who had trained since childhood in a specialist field, like athletes, were unwilling to get their hands dirty, were dreamers, luxury items or collateral in a culture war, was felt as a gross insult.

For the most recent alumni and current students of the Academy, the practical, political and philosophical fallout from lockdown was immense, as Freeman-Attwood and Elizabeth Kenny, Dean of Students, and one of the first musicians to perform in Wigmore Hall's livestreamed summer season, acknowledge. Freeman-Attwood was aware of what he describes as 'an ebb and flow of enthusiasm, support and also deep anxiety' in the first few months.

He began to write weekly bulletins to the whole community of students and staff, drawing everyone together and addressing issues such as the inevitable changes in the student experience and access to teaching while also talking about 'what it means to be a musician'. He was deeply concerned about those at the beginning of their careers – the freelance oboists or percussionists who might be third or fourth on the list to call for a job in good times and who had left education too recently to have sufficient tax records to qualify for government support – and was in close contact with trustees and key donors to reassure them that everything possible was being done to protect the institution, its staff, students and its international reputation. Meanwhile Kenny, who had recruited a third senior psychological therapist onto her team of counsellors, began sifting through the requests for logistical and pastoral assistance. The Students' Union and Student

Support Service were, in her words, 'front and centre' in the Academy's response to the crisis.

'There were certain things that created, over the summer, particular periods of collegiality and other things where people clearly felt that the whole world had disappeared from under them', says Freeman-Attwood. 'I think it would be very disingenuous not to identify the deep concern that a lot of students and staff had – and pastoral support became a key priority. Above all, we knew we had to stand our ground and advocate musicians as a community of enormous value to the world. The hopes were that new perspectives on change and opportunity would emerge without, as yet, knowing specifically where they would come from. Not being given any sense at all of the value in which the arts are held in this country, not just in an economic way but in terms of the fabric of society and its recovery, was unhelpful and demoralising. But I think young people are very idealistic about the value of what they do, whether it's because they've inherited certain ideals from their teachers and their mentors or just the way they're made. I find that totally inspirational and it makes us all want to make things work better and develop a curriculum which reflects the changing artistic needs of the age.'

Major concert projects for the summer term were shelved. The Musical Theatre Department pulled rehearsals for its annual agents showcase and began instead to train the company of singer-actors in self-filming songs and monologues for auditions: a practice common in film, television and theatre today. The gambit was successful and the majority of performers now have representation. Acting independently, groups of students posted their music on social-media platforms, playing in kitchens, front rooms and bedrooms under the banner #RAMplaysON. So great was the volume of video performances from players in the Brass, Woodwind, Strings, Piano and Vocal Studies Departments that it soon became impossible to list them all in one weekly email. Akugbo and his peers released a pitch-perfect split-screen video of Leroy Anderson's 1954 party piece, 'Bugler's Holiday', with a running joke in which one player kept losing his place in the music. At the time of writing, it has been seen by an audience of 1,037,764.

Stills from 'Bugler's Holiday', a video recorded and performed by Academy brass students during lockdown

Above: Still of a trombone
soloist performing in the Big
Band concert of music by Stan
Sulzmann, livestreamed from
the Susie Sainsbury Theatre

Left: Stills from 'Bugler's
Holiday', a video recorded and
performed by Academy brass
students during lockdown

As Kenny observes, 'motivation comes and goes in the middle of a global crisis'. Not everyone wants to be sharing their work on social media for likes and retweets. With teaching moved online, the focus shifted to the final recitals, normally held in May and early June of each year. As soon as the Academy reopened on 19 June 2020, the space was given over to the final-year students, undergraduate and postgraduate, to rehearse their programmes in the David Josefowitz Recital Hall, the Angela Burgess Recital Hall, the Duke's Hall and the Susie Sainsbury Theatre. 'It was very important for morale, I think,' says Freeman-Attwood, 'and especially as they were all streamed for parents and friends to watch their loved ones all over the world'. The last of 250 assessments took place forty-eight hours before the induction process of the new academic year began. It was Kenny's first year sitting on the panel and she recalls turning to her colleagues and asking whether the standard was normally this high.

'If we're thinking about what lessons can be learned from this experience, one huge lesson is that you can put on the most amazing array of activities that reflect the changing landscape of genres in terms of what people play and listen to and how they engage with other artists, but when it comes down to it, people need time to practise', says Freeman-Attwood. 'Many really got under the bonnet of their technical work during lockdown. It was no coincidence that heads of departments almost universally reported pleasant surprises from a large proportion of students who received marks well above expectations. Now the challenge is to recalibrate the programmes of study and ask whether the balance is as good as it could be. And whether we just make too many collective demands on students which can be counterproductive. It's an endless debate but Covid-19 has really brought it into focus.'

Neither Freeman-Attwood nor Kenny is comfortable with framing the experience of lockdown as a positive one. It has, however, stimulated a reassessment of priorities at the Academy and a reboot of core values and ethics. There is added impetus for advocacy of music in what has seemed at times like a hostile environment. Some

historical social issues were already being addressed before
March – problems with overt or unconscious bias over
gender and race, and concerns about equality of access
and opportunity in an industry that is generally assumed
to be liberal, if complacent in its liberalism – and how they
extend to safeguarding in the broadest sense. When the
Black Lives Matter movement found its platform in the
UK in June, the Academy stepped up its efforts to address
bias and representation in the curriculum, engaging the
Stephen Lawrence Trust to audit how the institution can be
more inclusive. 'We are also reviewing many fundamental
areas such as how we use our space, not just financially, but
educationally. These were things we were looking at before
Covid but they have now been intensified in our planning
and imagination', says Freeman-Attwood.

An epilogue is traditionally a means of neatly tying up
various threads of a narrative. This is not that. With a blended
model of in-person and online teaching as the year begins,
and an ambitious schedule of streamed performances,
the Academy is in transition, as is the industry for which
its students are training. It remains an international
community and an international project, as music always
has been.

Kenny was concerned that new and existing students
would be anxious about the possibility of another lockdown
and further disruption, but instead has found that the
atmosphere in the building, with its counterpoint between
old and new spaces, is positive. 'The psychological effect of,
potentially, not being able to start a new year was something
we had to reckon with, but that was helped enormously by
new students and our determination to do as much as we
can in person and in collective ensembles. That's why I'm
going in! It's because it is a shot in the arm to see people who
are all wearing masks but are all doing their stuff, and it's
great. It really is', she says.

'They're bringing in new energy, so that mitigates the
disappointment that the virus is now something we're
having to think of as a long haul. I think we'll always be
champing at the bit to come out of this constraining period
the second we can, and we won't go back into it until we
have to. If students are anxious, we can be sensitive and
flexible. In the building it's actually incredibly calm, so I
think Covid has made us recalibrate our view of life slightly.
There's buzz and there's energy and that's great, but actually
a bit of calm as well is quite good for everyone. I think that's
good for everyone's mental health.'

'In the building it's actually incredibly calm, so I think Covid has made us recalibrate our view of life slightly. There's buzz and there's energy and that's great, but actually a bit of calm as well is quite good for everyone.'

↖ Angela Burgess Recital Hall
↖ Susie Sainsbury Theatre Dress Circle
↖ Duke's Hall Balcony
↖ Henry Wood Room

ROYAL ACADEMY OF MUSIC AWARDS / IAN RITCHIE ARCHITECTS LTD

The Royal Academy of Music has won twenty-two awards (including RIBA National Award and London Building of the Year, AJ Retrofit Project of the Year and the British Construction Industry Project of the Year) and has been commended or shortlisted for a further twenty-four awards.

RAM Awards

Award Wins

2018	RIBA National Award
2018	RIBA London Building of the Year Award
2018	RIBA London Award
2018	RICS London Award – Leisure & Tourism
2018	NLA Award – Culture & Community
2018	AJ Retrofit Awards – Overall Winner UK Retrofit Project of the Year
2018	AJ Retrofit Awards – Cultural Buildings – Performance and Events
2018	British Construction Industry Awards – Cultural & Leisure Project of the Year
2018	London Construction Awards – London Build Excellence
2018	Wood Awards UK – Interiors
2018	FX Awards – Public Sector
2018	AJ Architecture Awards – Higher Education Project of the Year
2018	Architecture Masterprize (USA) – Educational Buildings
2018-19	International Property Awards – 'Leisure Architecture' UK region
2019	Civic Trust Award
2019	USITT (United States Institute for Theatre Technology) – Architecture Merit Award
2019	AJ Specification Awards – Fit-out & Interior
2019	World Architecture Community WA Awards 30th Cycle Winner
2019	Institute of Acoustics Peter Lord Award
2019	The Westminster Society Biennial Award 2019 – Renovated Architecture
2019	Chicago Athenaeum/The European Centre International Architecture Award
2019	Timber Trades Journal (TTJ) Timber Interiors Fit-out Award

Award Commendations & Shortlistings

2013	NLA Award – Conservation and Retrofit – Shortlist
2017	AR Future Project Awards – Old & New – Commended
2017	World Architecture Festival Awards – Education (Future Projects) – Shortlist
2018	World Architecture Festival Awards – Best Use of Certified Timber – Highly Commended
2018	World Architecture Festival Awards – Higher Education & Research (Completed) – Shortlist
2018	World Architecture News Awards – Performing Spaces – Shortlist
2018	Blueprint Awards – Shortlist
2018	ABB Leaf Awards – Shortlist
2018	AIA UK Design Excellence Awards – Shortlist
2018	ANC Acoustic Awards – Building Acoustics – Commended
2018	LUX Awards – Hospitality, Leisure and Faith Project of the Year – Commended
2018	London Construction Awards – Interior Design of the Year – Shortlist
2018	Blueprint Awards – Best Public Use Project – Shortlist
2019	Civic Trust Awards – Selwyn Goldsmith Award – Shortlist
2019	Surface Design Awards – Light and Surface Interior – Shortlist
2019	Surface Design Awards – Public Building Interior – Shortlist
2019	EU Prize for Contemporary Architecture – Mies van der Rohe Award – Nominee
2019	Offsite Awards – Installer of the Year – Shortlist
2019	Offsite Awards – Education Project of the Year – Shortlist
2019	Architizer A+ Awards – Cultural: Hall / Theatre – Finalist
2019	Timber Trades Journal (TTJ) Public or Commercial Use of Timber in Construction Award – High Commendation
2019	Structural Steel Design Awards – Commendation
2019	WAF World Building of the Year – Shortlist
2019	AR New into Old Awards – Shortlist
2020	The PLAN Awards (Italy) – Education (Completed Projects) – Honourable Mention

IAN RITCHIE ARCHITECTS LTD DESIGN AND CONSTRUCTION TEAMS

Architect and Principal Designer
Ian Ritchie Architects Ltd
José Garrido
Brian Heron
Jonathan Shaw

Cost Consultant
Equals Consulting

Structural Engineer
WSP Structures

Building Services
Atelier Ten (Stages D-L [3-7])
King Shaw Associates (Stages
A-C [0-2])

Acoustic Consultant
Arup Acoustics

Stage Theatre Consultant
Fisher Dachs Associates

Lighting Consultant
Ulrike Brandi Licht

Heritage Consultant
Donald Insall Associates

Access Consultant
Centre for Accessible
Environments

Fire Consultant
WSP Fire

Transport Consultant
WSP Transport

Approved Inspector
Approved Inspector
Services Ltd

Client Advisor
RISE

CONTRACTORS &
SUBCONTRACTORS

Main Contractor
Geoffrey Osborne Ltd

Joinery
James Johnson & Co. Ltd

Copper Roofing
All Metal Roofing

Fibre Optics / Crystals
Roblon

Glazing
Novum

Isolation Bearings
Farrat Isolevel Ltd

Metalwork
Structural Stairways Ltd

Piling
Keller Geotechnique Ltd

Services
Bradgate

Steelwork
Structural Steelcraft Ltd

Secondary Steelwork
Fabrite Engineering Ltd

Theatre Electrical Systems
Push The Button

Theatre Seating
Figueras

Theatre Rigging
Glantre Engineering Ltd

Groundworker / Blockwork
Macai

Acoustic Glazed Screens
Quietstar

Specialist Acoustic Doors
Safedoor

PICTURE CREDITS

Thank you to the following sources for providing the images featured in this book:

Front and back cover, and pp. 2, 4, 6, 9, 10, 12, 14, 27 (left), 31, 34, 42 (bottom), 43 (bottom), 43 (top), 44 (top), 44 (bottom), 45, 58 (top), 58 (bottom), 59 (top), 59 (bottom), 60 (top), 60 (bottom), 61, 62, 63, 66, 69, 72, 85, 88, 160, 176, 177, 190–1, 193, 194, 197, 198, 206–7: Adam Scott

pp. 16, 18 (left) 18 (centre), 18 (right), 19 (left), 19 (right), 20 (left), 20 (right), 21 (left), 21 (right), 22, 23, 24 (left), 24 (right), 25 (right), 25 (left), 26 (left), 27 (right), 28, 30, 36, 52, 53, 80, 90, 91, 94, 100, 111, 115 (top), 115 (bottom), 122, 124, 136, 142, 146–7, 163, 170, 172: Royal Academy of Music

pp. 26 (right), 79, 92, 102, 130 (right), 131, 132, 138, 148, 152: Robert Workman

pp. 32, 74: Jake Wiltshire

pp. 37, 38, 39 (bottom left), 39 (top right), 39 (bottom right), 40, 42 (top), 46 (left),

46 (right) 54 (top), 54 (bottom), 55, 56, 64 (left), 64 (right), 65, 68 (bottom), 68 (top), 200–1: Ian Ritchie Architects Ltd

p. 47 (top): Andreas Krumwiede/ Shutterstock

p. 47 (bottom): Jonathan P. McKinley

p. 49: Tomasz Wojtowicz, www.woodforguitar.com

p. 50: Adrian Borda/ Dreamstime.com

pp. 70, 71: Glantre Engineering Ltd

pp. 76, 81, 86, 89, 103 (left), 103 (right), 104, 114, 118, 135: Simon Jay Price

pp. 78, 101, 134, 145 (top): Harry Cole

pp. 82 (left), 82 (right), 83, 90 (left), 98, 112, 123, 126, 144, 178: Frances Marshall

pp. 84, 145 (bottom): Chris Christodoulou

p. 96: Sisi Burn

pp. 97, 173: Clive Barda/ArenaPAL

pp. 107, 108: Ben Tomlin Photography

pp. 130 (centre), 130 (left), 164: © Sarah Hickson

p. 143: Fred MacGregor/ Camera Press

pp. 149, 150, 156, 166, 180: Marc Brenner

p. 182: Will Upton

pp. 186, 187 (left and middle): 'Bugler's Holiday' from a video produced by Will Thomas

pp. 187 (right), 188, 189: Stills from the Royal Academy of Music YouTube channel

Every effort has been made to trace copyright holders and acknowledge the images. The publisher welcomes further information regarding any unintentional omissions.

INDEX

Published in 2021 by
Unicorn, an imprint of
Unicorn Publishing Group LLP
5 Newburgh Street
London
W1F 7RG
www.unicornpublishing.org

Text © Royal Academy of Music

Author
Anna Picard

Contributors
Jonathan Freeman-Attwood
Timothy Jones
Kirsty MacDonald
Ian Ritchie
Susie Sainsbury

ISBN 978-1-912690-72-5

10 9 8 7 6 5 4 3 2 1

Project manager and copy-editor
Linda Schofield

Design
Kathrin Jacobsen

Picture researcher
Katie Greenwood

Indexer
Elizabeth Wise

Printed in the EU

Front cover
Double bass student Joe Prindl
in the Angela Burgess Recital Hall

Back cover
Susie Sainsbury Theatre

Pages 2–3
Susie Sainsbury Theatre

Page 4
Façade of the Royal Academy
of Music

Pages 6–7, 206–7
Façade of the Royal Academy of Music,
view from Marylebone Road

Pages 190–1
The stained-glass window of the main
staircase, entitlted 'Victory', designed and
fabricated by Leonard Walker and unveiled
by Dame Myra Hess on 25 July 1946

Pages 200–1
Foyer of the Susie Sainsbury Theatre